"Within an hour of finishing this book, I found myself using some of the things I had learned. I recommend it to anyone who has ever wanted to help a friend who was hurting but didn't know what to do or say."

*Rev. Darren Walker*
*First United Methodist Church*
*Glen Rose, Texas*

"Dr. Haugk draws on his own pain, as well as research with thousands of others, to offer simple, practical ways to relate to those who are suffering."

*Sandy Gagliardi*
*St. Luke's Episcopal Church*
*Hilton Head Island, South Carolina*

"We are all called to care. This book provides the critical tools, understanding, and compassion we need to be a help and comfort to others. A must-read for everyone!"

*Michael L. Russo*
*St. Rochus Catholic Parish*
*Johnstown, Pennsylvania*

"No fluff, just compelling reading on the art of intelligent sensitivity toward those who are suffering."

*Dr. Mary Ann Bowman*
*First Presbyterian Church*
*Sarasota, Florida*

"This book stands head and shoulders above any other on how to care for those who suffer. Its warm, practical approach shows us how we can be Jesus Christ Incarnate to hurting people."

*Barbara Lambert*
*Altamesa Church of Christ*
*Fort Worth, Texas*

"Dr. Haugk has done it again! This very practical book will make a great difference to anyone walking alongside someone who is suffering."

*Rev. James B. Lambeth*
*Western Boulevard Presbyterian Church*
*Raleigh, North Carolina*

"At last! Concrete examples of what to say and what NOT to say."

*Shirley A. Marx*
*Village Green Baptist Church*
*Wheaton, Illinois*

"The careful use of personal examples gives this book humanity and humility."

*Rev. Robert J. Knepel*
*Immanuel Lutheran Church*
*East Aurora, New York*

"The tone is warm and inviting. I laughed. I cried. I marveled at how simple yet profound a caregiving relationship can be."

*Marjorie Tonole*
*Gold Canyon United Methodist Church*
*Clackamas, Oregon*

"I know this book is intended for caregivers, but I read it during a time of great suffering. It was a Godsend. Its message is gentle, yet right on target."

*Dee Coover*
*First Congregational Church*
*Hamden, Connecticut*

"This book will be a classic!"

*Dr. Ruth Winters*
*Crestwood United Methodist Church*
*Crestwood, Kentucky*

# DON'T SING SONGS TO A HEAVY HEART

# Also by Kenneth C. Haugk

# DON'T SING SONGS TO A HEAVY HEART

## HOW TO RELATE TO THOSE WHO ARE SUFFERING

KENNETH C. HAUGK, Ph.D.

STEPHEN MINISTRIES • ST. LOUIS, MISSOURI

## Don't Sing Songs to a Heavy Heart
### How to Relate to Those Who Are Suffering

ISBN: 1930445121

Library of Congress Catalog Card Number 2004112156

All Scripture quotations, unless otherwise noted, are from the Holy Bible, New International Version®. NIV®. Copyright © 1973, 1978, 1984 by the International Bible Society. Used by permission of Zondervan Publishing House. All rights reserved.

Scripture quotations marked NRSV are from the New Revised Standard Version of the Bible, copyright © 1989 by the Division of Christian Education of the National Council of the Churches of Christ in the USA and used by permission.

Printed in the U.S.A.

09  08  07  06  05  04
 6   5   4   3   2   1

*To Joan,*
*You light up my life.*

# CONTENTS

# Introduction

## FROM MANY HEARTS

On a warm day in early August, my wife Joan was first diagnosed with ovarian cancer, confirmed the next day by an oncologist. For Joan it was the beginning of her 41-month fight for life.

It was combat that took place with knives and poisons.

Amid all that flashing steel and the drip-drip-drip of deadly potions, we both learned a good deal about caring. We learned what helped and what didn't. We cringed at the remarks of some and glowed with warmth at the quality of caring and relating by others.

Years before, Joan and I had founded a training organization—Stephen Ministries—that has equipped hundreds of thousands of caregivers. Yet again and again during Joan's fierce fight to live, it was driven home to me that relating to those who are suffering is no small challenge.

One time, I sat with her through a whole afternoon while she cried. Just being with her—that was the right thing to do. She felt better. And you might think that all that follows, therefore, will be triumphal accounts of my educated and superior caregiving. Sorry. This book is about human beings, and all of us—myself included—have room to grow in this area.

Shel Silverstein's poem "Helping" defines two very different kinds of help:

> *And some kind of help*
> *Is the kind of help*
> *That helping's all about.*
>
> *And some kind of help*
> *Is the kind of help*
> *We all can do without.*[1]

I learned about both these kinds of helping in the almost three and a half years I spent with Joan in her struggle. And I changed. It became a lot easier for me to express my emotions. This was very good. I remember a call from a friend whose wife was also seriously ill. Shortly before Joan died he called to tell me his wife had died. I cried. This was exactly right for both of us at that time. I'm getting better at being in touch with my humanness. I haven't arrived yet, but I'd like to think I'm moving in the right direction.

Joan died on a cold January day.

In the face of someone else's great need, *everyone intends well.* No one plans to add to another person's hurt. We look for ways, you and I, to console, to comfort, to express our care and love from the depths of our hearts. And if we are the hurting person, we hope for consolation, comfort, care, and love that will reach our hearts even when we feel most unreachable.

I began notes for this book in San Antonio, Texas, while

Joan was in the hospital on two occasions for a total of 47 days. I stayed with her, sleeping on a cot in her room. We had journeyed there from St. Louis to participate in a clinical trial, an experimental treatment for her cancer.

The first trip to San Antonio was supposed to last only ten days, just long enough for Joan to go through the preliminaries and receive two of the experimental treatments. After that, we had intended to commute from St. Louis to San Antonio for ongoing treatments. But we ended up staying in San Antonio for three months and nine days. Our plans changed abruptly because the cancer had progressed further than we thought. As one thing led to another—chemotherapy, surgery, two bouts with infections—I was rarely apart from Joan. Because she slept quite a lot, I had a good deal of time to reflect and write.

I had some hunches about what was helpful, not so helpful, and even downright harmful. These hunches were greatly validated by Joan, the rest of our family, and some friends and acquaintances who themselves had gone through or were going through a variety of experiences of deep pain and suffering. But hunches alone were not quite good enough, not quite sufficient. They needed to be tested, to be researched in a systematic way.

The fragile vulnerability of those who are suffering is what made me so determined to research these concepts of caring and relating. The subject matter, but more importantly, the people who are suffering, deserve it. There's more than enough pain in the world to go around. I wanted to alleviate some of that pain by heading off the hurtful and promoting the helpful.

To do this I assembled a research team to investigate via individual interviews, focus groups, and surveys the many facets of relating to those who are suffering. Some of the research was from the perspective of caregivers, but the vast majority was conducted with individuals who shared from the depths of their own pain and suffering—past and sometimes present. In all, a total of 4,252 individuals participated in this research.

These people opened their hearts. They answered scores of specific questions. This was more than an exercise for them—it was personal! Most of the time my own instincts and reactions about good and bad caregiving turned out to be true for others as well, but not always. There were some surprises, too. After an immense amount of distilling, sorting, and tallying, patterns emerged, patterns tested in the fires of people's experiences.

The result is this book, which comes to you out of the fire—from my heart, and from many hearts.

# 1

# THE CALL TO CARE

*Dear God, I wish everything about relationships were easier. Sometimes I wish you would hurry up and finish perfecting me, so I would always know what to do or say when someone needs comfort. No challenges, no problems. But I know better. Thank you for being with me in real life, for helping me grow. Amen.*

No one sets out in the morning saying, "Today I'm going to add to the pain that my friend Charlie is feeling by making some insensitive comments to him about his dying wife." Or "Today I'm going to add to Anne's suffering by being insufferably cheerful during my visit with her." Right along with everyone else, you want to be a good caregiver to those who are suffering.

For a while I belonged to a local association of psychologists who met monthly for dinner, followed by a short business meeting and then a program. At one point, the wife of the association president was in the later stages of cancer. After spending the afternoon and early part of the evening at the hospital with his wife, he arrived at the meeting just in time to have a cup of coffee with the rest of us after dinner. As he was taking his seat, someone asked him how his wife was doing. He responded simply, "She's dying."

One of the other psychologists said to him, "We're all dying." At the time, this psychologist was teaching a university course on the subject of death and dying. Her statement was 100% accurate—we are all dying. This is a profound truth. But just because a statement is true does not make it helpful. Her statement—no matter how true or profound—was not what the association president needed to hear at that time. This was clearly evidenced by his immediate scowl and stone-cold silence.

Everyone at times misses the mark—sometimes even the whole target! Friends, acquaintances, highly trained professionals, religious people, lovers to their beloveds, you, me—everyone who means to offer comfort sometimes manages instead to pile more weight on an already heavily burdened heart.

## PROVERBIAL WISDOM

The writers of the Bible were well aware of this human tendency to add to the pain of those we really want to help. The Book of Proverbs, a collection of wise sayings about what is generally true in life, was used to instruct and guide people how to live. One proverb in particular speaks directly to the purpose of this book:

> *Like one who takes away a garment on a cold day,*
> *or like vinegar poured on soda,*
> *is one who sings songs to a heavy heart.*

> *—Proverbs 25:20*

Paraphrased, the passage could read like this: As uncaring as it is to rip off someone's coat on a cold day, as messy as it becomes when you pour vinegar on baking soda, you can expect the same kind of results if you say cheery things to a person with a heavy heart.

*Heavy heart* describes the feelings of a person who is disappointed or depressed, sorrowful or ill, experiencing some kind of trouble, misfortune, or distress. This proverb isn't telling caregivers that they should avoid music around someone with a heavy heart. Instead, it speaks about the false cheeriness of caregivers who gloss over the sufferer's pain. Though it might seem that you could lighten a heavy heart by "singing songs" to it—by uttering lighthearted words or sunny phrases—the chances are great that you'll only make things worse.

Those who sing cheery songs to heavy hearts abandon suffering people to bear their burdens alone. No one understands. No one acknowledges their pain. This passage from Proverbs—as true today as ever—says that you can actually increase a suffering person's pain with misdirected care. With the best of intentions you can add to people's problems. Suffering individuals who hear such "songs" may feel worse because they reason, *Everyone thinks I should be better (happy, bearing up, improving), but I'm not. What's the matter with me?*

Some Christians double the impact of this false reasoning by teaching that Christians are supposed to be happy all the time. This impossible expectation can lead suffering Christians into habitual hypocrisy, pretending to be happy when they're not. Since they're taught to do so, they hide their real feelings. Feigning cheerfulness saps energy and causes people to miss the chance to experience true joy. By not allowing themselves to experience the depths of their emotions, they also miss out on experiencing the heights.

## CHALLENGES

Those who are suffering are very vulnerable. It's as though they have been stamped FRAGILE, HANDLE WITH CARE. Because suffering people are so fragile, those who relate to them are called upon to function with the greatest sensitivity and compassion they can muster. This is where the challenge lies.

And the *challenge* of relating becomes many challenges. Identifying exactly what those challenges are was one of the first tasks of our research. We asked caregivers to tell what they thought were their greatest difficulties in relating to those who are suffering. We also asked those who had received care to share what they perceived others' difficulties were in relating to them. Both caregiver and care receiver respondents shared freely and fully. Here is what they reported, in order of frequency, as major challenges.

1. Knowing what to say to a hurting person
2. Understanding, empathizing with, or validating someone's struggles
3. Talking too much, listening too little
4. Having a "fix-it" mentality
5. Feeling discomfort in the face of someone's pain
6. Focusing on self rather than the hurting person

7. Wanting people to "get over it"

8. Avoiding painful subjects

9. Avoiding hurting persons

10. Giving advice, being too directive

11. Minimizing the significance of the pain or suffering

12. Being judgmental

13. Wanting to hear only the positive

14. Responding with clichés, platitudes, or pat phrases

15. Identifying too closely with the other's pain

16. Feeling helpless

17. Handling the anger of those who are suffering

18. Knowing what would be intrusive or welcomed

19. Getting people to open up

This is a formidable list, certainly, but not an insurmountable one. The items on this list are interrelated, which is good news, because as you overcome one area of challenge, it will positively affect other areas as well. Mastering these challenges and turning them into opportunities to relate well to suffering people is what this book is all about.

## GOALS OF THIS BOOK

The primary purpose of this book is to examine very carefully what to say and do in relating to people who have heavy hearts. The goal is not only to say, "Don't sing songs to heavy hearts," but also to lay out all the constructive things you *can* say and do. By your effective caring and relating, hurting people will experience the warmth of being cared for, and their hearts may even be lightened. You will stand out as refreshingly different in your relating to those who are suffering.

This book also has an equipping goal that goes beyond what you should or shouldn't do or say in your caregiving. I hope it will also change you from the inside out. Who you are as a person is your main resource for caring and relating. As your own heart is changed, your caring and relating will reflect the difference.

You've no doubt seen the popular slogan: "Please be patient. God isn't finished with me yet." It's popular because it's true. One of the great truths about relating to those who are suffering is that nobody does it perfectly. But God continues to call imperfect people to reach out and do the best we can. Realizing that it's all right to be a work in progress frees us to care even as we continue to grow in those areas where we are still "unfinished." The fact that you are reading this book indicates that you are serious about caring well for hurting people.

As Christians, God has charged us with a special mission of love, and times of suffering call for the best we can bring in hope and in compassion. My prayer is that, after you've read this book, you will feel better equipped and ready to offer hope and compassion to people with heavy hearts.

# 2

# A BIBLICAL UNDERSTANDING
# OF SUFFERING

*Open my mind, O Lord, to the influence of your blessed Word. Teach me what you would have me know about suffering. Let knowledge chase away my preconceptions and misconceptions, and let love animate the understanding I gain. This I ask in the name of your Son, Jesus. Amen.*

The fabric of the Bible consists of various strands and threads—family histories and national archives, letters and poetry, epic battles and love stories—all woven together in a remarkable tapestry that features a loving God who cares for *real people*. The Bible portrays these real people in living color, with their complex personalities, strained relationships, and a variety of problems. We can learn a great deal about pain and suffering from its pages—comfort for those who suffer and wisdom for those who care.

The Bible portrays suffering realistically, not as if all problems can be resolved and loose ends tied up neatly like in a television drama. Life isn't all sweetness and light. People in the Bible faced the full gamut of human experience and emotion, from glory and joy to struggles, despair, and ruin. Scripture talks about real people with real challenges, real heartaches, and real suffering.

Many people think of Job as the epitome of misery in the Bible. He lost his children, his wealth, his health. Job's story is powerful, but he is not alone. In fact, significant suffering touched most of the men and women whom God singled out by special call. Abraham and Sarah's infertility caused severe distress and led to marital strain. Moses was an outcast for forty years—rejected by both Egyptians and Hebrews. Further, the driving goal and ambition of Moses' life—to lead God's people to the promised land of Israel—was left unfulfilled. David endured repeated attempts on his life, the untimely death of his best friend, the death of an infant, the murder of one son at the hands of another son, and the death of a rebellious son. An unnamed "thorn in the flesh" troubled the apostle Paul. These pillars of the faith—and many others who were much loved by God—still experienced profound suffering.

And then, of course, there was Jesus himself—a man of sorrows, well acquainted with pain and suffering.

## ALREADY AND NOT YET

*The Bible speaks:*

> Now if we are children, then we are heirs—heirs of God and co-heirs with Christ, if indeed we share in his sufferings in order that we may also share in his glory. I consider that our present

sufferings are not worth comparing with the glory
that will be revealed in us. . . . We know that the
whole creation has been groaning as in the pains
of childbirth right up to the present time. . . .
And we know that in all things God works for the
good of those who love him, who have been
called according to his purpose (Romans
8:17–18, 22, 28).

Romans 8 is an absolutely wonderful chapter that gives a
wide perspective and a deep understanding of the Christian
life. In this chapter Paul lays out the whole panorama of the
Christian's life with God—past, present, and future.

Verse 28 of that chapter—"And we know that in all things
God works for the good of those who love him"—is an
absolutely wonderful verse. As with any passage of
Scripture, however, it's important to pay careful attention to
its context and to what it does and does not say. Does Paul
say that *in this lifetime*—sometime between the cradle and
the grave—everything will turn out right? He doesn't even
say that everything will make sense in this lifetime.

In fact, Paul is not talking about the narrow span of
human life on earth but the widest possible perspective of
God's plans and purposes for human beings and the whole
creation. This chapter is God's eye view of life, an eternal
perspective.

Romans 8:28 can be a problem when shared with hurting
people apart from its context of suffering with Jesus, creation groaning, and waiting in expectation for a better time.
This verse offers hope, but not immediate relief. There is
hope in knowing that your present sufferings are temporary

and that they are not without meaning. But this hope doesn't make present hurts go away.

Paul says that the believer's situation is like that of a mother giving birth: "We know that the whole creation has been groaning as in the pains of childbirth right up to the present time" (Romans 8:22). What an appropriate image! A mother giving birth knows intellectually that her labor pains are temporary. She eagerly anticipates relief from pain and looks forward to welcoming her child joyfully into the world. Yet no sensitive person—not to mention any mother who has given birth—would ever imagine that this knowledge and hope provide immediate relief from the mother's labor pains. Hope does not negate pain. The hope of Romans 8:28 is not intended to be a panacea for the groaning of Romans 8:22. That would be totally inconsistent for Paul, who four chapters later in Romans 12:15 says, "Rejoice with those who rejoice; mourn with those who mourn."

As members of God's family, we Christians are heirs—not just because of what we already have, but also because of what we do not yet possess. For an heir, the future contains hope, the promise of an inheritance. For all the many blessings and benefits we already enjoy as God's children, the best is yet to come. Because the full glory of God's kingdom lies in the future, present reality remains tinged by pain and sorrow. This is why Paul can talk about "our present sufferings" in the same sentence in which he mentions "the glory that will be revealed in us" (v. 18). There is a real, unresolved tension between what we experience now in this life and the future hope we possess.

Although Christians are Christ's new creation now, we do not yet live in a totally renewed creation. The whole fallen creation must await its full restoration at Christ's return. For now, the Christian life still involves suffering (v. 18), frustration (v. 20), bondage to decay (v. 21), groaning (v. 22), and weakness (v. 26). Later (Romans 8:35) Paul observes that Christians may face trouble, hardship, persecution, famine, nakedness, danger, or sword. The life of a Christian is not all joy upon inexpressible joy. It is a sometimes confusing combination of joy and sadness, contentment and restlessness, comfort and pain. Many longed-for benefits of being God's heir are delayed, including freedom from pain and suffering. The "not yet"—the future hope—gives a context to the Christian's present pain and suffering.

*The Bible speaks:*

> To keep me from becoming conceited . . . there was given me a thorn in my flesh, a messenger of Satan, to torment me. Three times I pleaded with the Lord to take it away from me. But he said to me, "My grace is sufficient for you, for my power is made perfect in weakness." Therefore I will boast all the more gladly about my weaknesses, so that Christ's power may rest on me. That is why, for Christ's sake, I delight in weaknesses, in insults, in hardships, in persecutions, in difficulties. For when I am weak, then I am strong (2 Corinthians 12:7–10).

What was Paul's "thorn in the flesh"? It is good Paul doesn't say. If he did, some might feel ashamed by their own inability to conquer lesser maladies. Others might feel superior to Paul: "Oh, is that all he had to deal with?" All we really need to know about Paul's thorn in the flesh is that it tormented him and he considered it a device of the evil one. Pain hurts—even for great men and women of faith.

The New Testament never asserts that faith is an insurance policy against suffering. God doesn't bargain people into faith in Jesus by offering them immunity from suffering. Because Jesus took on himself the punishment for our sins, we are free from sin's punishment, but not from life's suffering. Paul, as a child of God, had the hope of a suffering-free future, but he still experienced the pain of an imperfect world. He longed for relief he knew would one day be his, but could not be his right now.

Paul writes honestly about his life. He doesn't dwell on his successes. Instead he tells about his unrelieved pain so that his readers will hear what God says to him in response to his prayer: "My grace is sufficient for you, for my power is made perfect in weakness."

God doesn't initiate the pain in Paul's life, but he does redeem the pain. God gives Paul in his pain a richer understanding of grace—a grace that is sufficient to carry him through his suffering and to equip him to minister even more capably to others. Precisely because of his pain and suffering, Paul is able to share the love of Christ with others in a more genuine and empathic way.

Unfortunately, some quote this passage to hurting people in a way that hurting people feel dismisses their suffering—as if God's grace and power should numb their pain. God doesn't promise to remove pain. Instead, he offers grace that is sufficient to see them through the pain. Following Paul's

own model, the safest advice for quoting, "My grace is sufficient for you, for my power is made perfect in weakness,"
is that it is best uttered by people who are themselves suffering; second best by people who have suffered, but only about
their own suffering; and not at all by those who cannot
empathize with the suffering of others.

*The Bible speaks:*

> "He will wipe every tear from their eyes. There
> will be no more death or mourning or crying or
> pain, for the old order of things has passed away."
> He who was seated on the throne said, "I am mak-
> ing everything new!" (Revelation 21:4–5a).

John wrote the book of Revelation to Christians who had
every reason to believe the world was falling apart. The
seven churches to whom the book of Revelation was
addressed were small bands of Christians scattered throughout Asia Minor, dominated by the Roman Empire. Many
were facing persecution. At any moment, they expected their
lives would be changed suddenly and irrevocably. But John
looked beyond the dark clouds of impending threat to the
hope of God through Jesus Christ.

Instead of fixating on his rapidly deteriorating world,
John chose to focus on the hope of Jesus' resurrection and
new life. The resurrection of Jesus and the coming of the
Holy Spirit signaled the beginning of the church, but even
more to the point, it signaled the beginning of God's new
creation—his grand restoration project.

While God is actively re-creating, there are still tears and
death, mourning and sadness, pain and suffering. But Jesus

offers the sure hope that one day there will be no more pain and suffering. The old order will pass away, and behold, all things will be new. In the midst of suffering, Christians have the promise that someday God "will wipe every tear from their eyes. There will be no more death or mourning or crying or pain." That's not an idea to be flung blindly at those who are hurting. It's a message that each Christian needs to claim, ponder, pray over, cherish, and live by.

The church's unique mission belongs to the transitional period between the beginning of the new creation at the first Easter and its final completion at the end of time. Christians are Easter people. You are an Easter person—you know the transforming power of Jesus Christ that renews and re-creates. But very often the world looks less like Easter and more like Good Friday. Rather than resurrection or rebirth, hurting people may be experiencing the darkness of a personal Golgotha. As those who are suffering face their darkest hours, you can be the means through which God begins to wipe away their tears.

The community of believers—the church—is called to be Christ's Easter body in a Good Friday world. Through the church, the risen Christ is *already* alive and at work in our pain-filled, suffering world.

## Christ Caring for People through People

*The Bible speaks:*

> Even though I walk through the valley of the shadow of death, I will fear no evil, for you are with me; your rod and your staff, they comfort me (Psalm 23:4).

Perhaps no passage of Scripture has been used more often to comfort hurting people than Psalm 23. What comfort do the suffering find here? The incomparable presence of God.

In search of good pastureland, shepherds and sheep often encountered danger because of the rugged landscape, the constant threat of attack by wild animals, or the ruthlessness of robbers and bandits. As the shepherd and his sheep together entered the valley of the shadow of death, the shepherd carried a rod and staff to protect his sheep and himself from harm.

Just as the shepherd is with his sheep, God is with his people. His presence comforts. It means that wherever we are, in whatever situation, we are not alone.

Not alone! What is more discouraging and disorienting than feeling utterly alone? Jesus knew something about loneliness. The Trinity has been described as an ongoing and eternal conversation of love, a "with-ness" for which human companionship has no parallel. On the cross, Jesus suddenly experienced abandonment—the total disruption of this unique relationship. Those who suffer aloneness experience depths of despair poignantly expressed in Jesus' heartbreaking cry on the cross: "My God, my God, why have you forsaken me?"

Aloneness is never so sharp as when someone is suffering. While God's presence can be a powerful antidote to loneliness, suffering people may have a difficult time believing God is with them. One gift you can offer them is to be present in their pain. The physical presence of another human being can bring significant comfort to those who are suffering.

Even more helpful is to have someone with them in mind and spirit—understanding and empathizing with them in their pain. Even terrible pain and suffering can become bearable when people know someone is truly and fully with them. As a caring Christian, you follow the Good Shepherd's example when you walk with them in their dark valleys.

*The Bible speaks:*

> Praise be to the God and Father of our Lord Jesus Christ, the Father of compassion and the God of all comfort, who comforts us in all our troubles, so that we can comfort those in any trouble with the comfort we ourselves have received from God. For just as the sufferings of Christ flow over into our lives, so also through Christ our comfort overflows (2 Corinthians 1:3–5).

The Russian novelist Leo Tolstoy loved the workers on his family's estate, so for a while he worked with them and shared their food and slept in their primitive cottages. But he was shocked when the workers told him, "We're not really impressed by your coming to live like us. You've got your rich father to fall back on. You can stop living in poverty any time you choose. But this is just what we cannot do. You just *act* as if you were one of us."

As Christians, when we meet Jesus, we meet God in the flesh. Jesus did not merely *act* as if he were like us. He suffered like us and for us. He even experienced the sense of being godforsaken that we may feel when we suffer.

We are never alone in suffering because God suffers with us. The idea of a suffering God is distinctively Christian.

Perhaps because God is a suffering God, he is uniquely qualified to be the "Father of compassion and the God of all comfort." God is with us as one who understands pain and suffering from personal experience.

Paul's firm belief that God comforts his people in troubled times was truly revolutionary. In Paul's world, people believed that the gods didn't care at all about humans or their comfort. But Paul says we don't have to suffer alone because God is the source of all comfort.

The Greek word translated *comfort* has the basic meaning "to call alongside." When Jesus promised to send the Holy Spirit in John 14:26, he referred to the Spirit by the name "Comforter"—the one called to your side.

When Paul talks about the comfort of God, he speaks from experience, from a life full of troubles, afflictions, and pressures. If Paul offers any solace in this dangerous flurry of chaos called life, he's going to do it as one who's earned the right to speak.

Christians by definition are people who receive the comfort of God and are empowered to embody God's comfort in their relationships with others. We are called into a community of comforters, the church, at the head of which stands the suffering God, the source of all comfort.

*The Bible speaks:*

> No one has ever seen God; but if we love one another, God lives in us and his love is made complete in us (1 John 4:12).

When God chose to reveal himself to humanity, he did so in the way that we human beings are most capable of

understanding. He knew that men and women could experience his presence most powerfully, not through glimpses of
heaven or mystical visions, but in human form—in Jesus.

Throughout his life, Jesus exemplified care and compassion for those who were hurting. Christians are called to be
Christ to the world by incarnating his love wherever there is
pain and suffering. When Christians love and care for those
who are hurting, God's character shines forth. No one has
ever seen God, but they see God's love through caring and
compassionate Christians. Just as you can see God by what
Jesus did, so those who are suffering can see God by what
you do.

Suffering, especially if it's prolonged or severe, can cause
people to question God's presence and care. But if they can
feel his love, a love made incarnate, full and complete, in the
caring people they see, touch, and hear, then they are assured
of God's presence. They can know that he hasn't abandoned
them. In you they see God.

## THE FELLOWSHIP OF SUFFERING

*The Bible speaks:*

> So in Christ we who are many form one body, and
> each member belongs to all the others (Romans
> 12:5).

In Romans, Paul addresses a band of believers living in
the heart of a thriving empire. This cosmopolitan church was
certainly full of people with different backgrounds, experiences, gifts, abilities, and perspectives. Paul teaches that the
church is as diverse as the human body, with each member

offering a unique giftedness, performing a different role or function. But just like the human body, the body of Christ is unified in purpose. Believers are always part of something much larger than themselves. The idea of a lone or maverick Christian is not found in the New Testament. Instead, each Christian is united with all other Christians to form one body.

Paul makes clear: "If one part suffers, every part suffers with it; if one part is honored, every part rejoices with it" (1 Corinthians 12:26). Christians are beloved members of God's family—sons and daughters, brothers and sisters. Whatever joy or sorrow touches one family member affects all family members. This has always been true. If a daughter experiences a great success, the whole family is energized by her accomplishment. If a son loses a best friend, all family members are touched by his sadness and sense of loss. As a member of God's family, you are called to bear what the family bears, no less. That's how Paul describes the church as God intends it to be.

*The Bible speaks:*
> Rejoice with those who rejoice; mourn with those
> who mourn (Romans 12:15).

The church is designed to function as a community. Fellowship among the members of the church should be so deep that members function as one body. When your little toe hurts, your whole body feels the pain and takes measures to alleviate it. So it should be in the body of Christ. When one member is suffering, the most natural thing would be for other members of the body to feel the pain as well. Whatever emotions or feelings a believer experiences, other

Christians need to be right there to share in the joy or the sorrow. But don't expect a suffering person to send you an engraved invitation to come alongside. *You* need to take the initiative.

The actions Paul proposes—rejoicing or mourning— point to the need for empathy. *Empathy* means "feeling with." Note that Paul doesn't say, "Rejoice with those who rejoice, and also rejoice with those who mourn because it will get them to feel better." Instead, his words are powerful, clear-cut, and plainspoken. When someone is rejoicing, rejoice with the person. When someone is mourning, you mourn as well. Nowhere does it say in this passage—or in any other passage in the Bible—that it would be good to try to stop people from feeling and expressing their pain. Hurting people need caregivers who will match their mood to a certain extent—laugh with them when they feel like laughing and cry when they feel like crying. Remember how Jesus wept with Mary and Martha at the tomb of Lazarus. Christians who mourn with those who mourn are following the pattern of Jesus Christ and incarnating his love to the hurting.

*The Bible speaks:*

> I want to know Christ and the power of his resurrection and the fellowship of sharing in his sufferings, becoming like him in his death, and so, somehow, to attain to the resurrection from the dead (Philippians 3:10–11).

You share in community when you participate in the sufferings of a brother or sister. But you also are called to participate or share in the sufferings of Christ. How can this happen? Didn't Jesus already experience his pain and suffering? How can you participate in it now?

On the cross, Jesus took upon himself all the sins and sorrows, all the pains and sufferings of the world. But as long as sickness and sadness remain, Jesus still suffers along with those he loves. He invites—no, expects—us to share in his suffering. We may not suffer exactly as Jesus did, or even as Paul; yet we will still suffer. Participation in Christ's suffering is not simply a one-time event that occurs at conversion and then becomes history. It is a daily, ongoing experience of personal devotion to Jesus.

Part of what it means to share in Christ's suffering is to share in the suffering of those whom Christ loves. You participate in Christ's sufferings by sharing the pain with those who suffer, not only fellow Christians, but people anywhere in the world who are hurting. You participate in Christ's sufferings when you come alongside the hurting and offer them the blessing of presence. You participate in Christ's sufferings when you weep with those who weep. You participate in Christ's sufferings when you die to yourself so that you can fully enter into the pain and suffering of another person.

You may never be more Christlike than when you participate in the sufferings and sorrows of a hurting world, wrestling with the pain and providing the comfort of community. Christ set the pattern: death, then rebirth; dying, then living again; suffering, then consolation. As you model the life of Christ in ministry to others, you become Christ to hurting people.

Jesus called his followers to pattern their lives after his, and that pattern includes dignifying pain and suffering. Pain is real, it hurts, and it matters. Rather than minimizing or denying the hurt, Christians are most like Christ when they enter into the pain of those who are suffering—not to be weighed down or consumed by it, but to help bear the burden. Jesus says that when you provide care in his name to the least of his brothers or sisters, you are having compassion on him (Matthew 25:31–40). So when you care for those in need, you are offering a doubly powerful witness to the presence of Christ in the world—Christ alive in you and in the one to whom you are offering care.

# 3

# A Guest in a Holy Place

*Dear God, I don't really want everyone to be just like me, but sometimes I think it sure would make life a lot easier. Help me honor the uniqueness of those who suffer and the uniqueness of their suffering. Guide me as I enter the place where they are. Teach me how to move toward understanding as I get to know each of them as individuals, even as Jesus knows me. Amen.*

When you offer care and comfort to another, you are stepping into a holy place, into the other person's unique universe of selfhood, need, and pain. It is holy because, when you enter in, you will find Jesus already there ahead of you—in that unique person. What a privilege!

You are entering another's house of pain.

When you enter another person's home, you know there are rules or customs of tradition, courtesy, and common sense. You are the guest. The other person is the host, and the host sets the rules, not you. For example, you don't presume to go wherever you want without asking. Parts of the house are private unless the host invites you to enter them. You follow rules of courtesy to be polite and well mannered in the home of another. And common sense tells you that you don't get to redecorate another person's house to suit your own taste.

As with homes, so it is with lives. Each hurting person is unique, each one an individual. The one who is hurting offers you the hospitality of his or her most private space, a room furnished with pain. As a guest in that private space, you should not attempt to redo the person's way of handling the situation to suit yourself.

The implication of this for you as a caring person is clear. Your every effort needs to be a loving attempt to perceive the depths of the other's suffering. Your task is to understand and appreciate the uniqueness of the person in front of you.

## WHO IS THE SUFFERER?

People have different life histories that affect how they handle crises and other life events that bring on pain and suffering. A few emerge from adversity as shining champions, standing tall amidst the rubble. The major league baseball player Lou Gehrig was one such stalwart.

Gehrig played first base for the New York Yankees from 1923 through early 1939 and was one of the first inductees into the Baseball Hall of Fame. During his time with the Yankees, he batted cleanup behind Babe Ruth and held the record for most consecutive games played—2,130—until Cal Ripken, Jr., of the Baltimore Orioles broke that record in 1995. Lou Gehrig was one of the greatest baseball players of all time, and at the very pinnacle of his career, he was

diagnosed with amyotrophic lateral sclerosis (ALS), a fatal
degenerative nerve disease that has since become known as
Lou Gehrig's Disease. He was forced to leave the game he
loved. Everyone who has heard or read his farewell speech
to 62,000 fans in Yankee Stadium on July 4, 1939, has been
moved by his fortitude and simple eloquence.

> Fans, for the past two weeks you have been read-
> ing about the bad break I got. Yet today I con-
> sider myself the luckiest man on the face of this
> earth. I have been in ballparks for seventeen years
> and have never received anything but kindness
> and encouragement from you fans. Look at these
> grand men. Which of you wouldn't consider it the
> highlight of his career just to associate with them
> for even one day? Sure I'm lucky. . . . When the
> New York Giants, a team you would give your
> right arm to beat, and vice versa, sends you a
> gift—that's something. When everybody down to
> the groundskeepers and those boys in white coats
> remember you with trophies—that's something.
> When you have a wonderful mother-in-law who
> takes sides with you in squabbles with her own
> daughter—that's something. When you have a
> father and a mother who work all their lives so
> you can have an education and build your body—
> it's a blessing. When you have a wife who has
> been a tower of strength and shown more courage
> than you dreamed existed—that's the finest I
> know. So I close in saying that I may have had a
> tough break, but I have an awful lot to live for.

Gehrig died less than two years later at the age of 37.

It's obvious from his words that Lou Gehrig was extremely blessed, even for a star major league baseball player. He received tremendous support throughout his life from his parents, his wife, and even his mother-in-law, not to mention the adulation of fans and fellow players during a baseball career that spanned 17 years with the Yankees. Despite a certain death sentence, he could stand before 62,000 people in Yankee Stadium and declare that he was "the luckiest man on the face of this earth." What a positive attitude! What a wonderful perspective! What appreciation of life!

It's a great temptation to cite this example or others as the "proper" way to cope with misfortune. But to think or, worse yet, to say to someone who has been diagnosed with ALS, "Lou Gehrig had ALS, and look how magnificently he handled it!" is cruelty at its worst.

Pointing to the way well-known people appear to deal with their suffering is very enticing. They often seem to handle their grief with great strength and stoicism, but no one knows what they are really feeling inside. Few people see what happens when the cameras stop rolling. It's essential not to judge a person for the way he or she is handling suffering nor to compare that person to anyone else, especially not to people in the public eye whose lives are often seen only in clips and cameos in the news.

Each person is socially conditioned over many years and by many experiences. That conditioning affects how he or she responds to life crises and other events that lead to suffering. People with the same kind of illness will respond to it differently because of the way their early learning experiences influence their current perception of the situation. One man said that he was told when growing up, "Pain and suffering are part of the human condition. Buck up and get through it and over it. You can do it; your parents, grandparents, uncles, aunts, and so on, have. There's nothing special or different about you. Get over it and move on." That person will respond quite differently to a painful event than another man who said he was taught to "share it, get it out, and not internalize it."

An individual's spiritual beliefs also condition his or her response to suffering. Some Christians are taught that God sends pain and suffering to people as punishment for their sins or to "help" them grow spiritually. That becomes the canvas upon which their lives are painted. How different is the life-canvas available to someone who can confidently say, "In all things, I know God will be with me. God will feel my pain and suffering and help me through it. God has promised never to leave me."

The ancient saints of legendary fortitude are often held up as examples of how Christians should act in painful situations. To ask a suffering person, "Why don't you have the patience (endurance, courage, faith . . .) of Job?" necessitates a simple and easy answer: "Because I'm not Job." Few understand that it took much time—and suffering—for these saints of old to reach the advanced level of faith to which hurting people are sometimes pointed.

Getting outside yourself and your own preconceptions about how a suffering person should respond isn't always easy. It calls for focusing on the hurting individual rather than on what you believe he or she should think or feel. If you can truly believe that every sufferer and every situation of suffering is unique, you will increase your chances of seeing with new eyes and hearing with new ears—and caring with new passion.

## WHAT IS THE SOURCE OF THE SUFFERING?

Pain and suffering may also be experienced as more or less difficult depending upon the nature of the event or crisis that caused it. Consider C. S. Lewis's reflections following the death of his wife, Joy.

> Getting over it so soon? But the words are ambiguous. To say the patient is getting over it after an operation for appendicitis is one thing; after he's had his leg off it is quite another. After that operation either the wounded stump heals or the man dies. If it heals, the fierce, continuous pain will stop. Presently he'll get back his strength and be able to stump about on his wooden leg. He has "got over it." But he will probably have recurrent pains in the stump all his life, and perhaps pretty bad ones; and he will always be a one-legged man. There will be hardly any moment when he forgets it. Bathing, dressing, sitting down and getting up again, even lying in bed, will all be different. His whole way of life will be changed. All sorts of pleasures and activities that he once took for granted will have to be simply written off. Duties too. At present I am learning to get about on crutches. Perhaps I shall presently be given a wooden leg. But I shall never be a biped again.[1]

"Getting over it"—whatever the pain or suffering is—will be influenced not only by how a person's life history shapes his or her perception of the pain, but also by the severity of the events leading to the suffering. Research respondents reported that the level of difficulty in handling a crisis or painful event increases if it

- is life-shortening
- is of longer duration or permanent
- leads to no recovery or only partial recovery
- involves great pain, physical or other
- produces multiple crises simultaneously
- requires significant lifestyle changes
- comes as a complete shock

As a caregiver, remember that each individual's suffering is uniquely difficult and can't be compared to any other person's experience. An individual's suffering shouldn't be minimized, for example, because it doesn't include any of the elements listed above. If the suffering person's experience does include one or more of the above factors, however, it is likely that his or her suffering will be greater than if those factors were not present.

## WHAT RESOURCES ARE AVAILABLE TO THE SUFFERER?

In addition to a person's prior life experiences and the type of crisis or life event leading to the suffering, the resources currently available to the sufferer also affect his or her ability to cope. Here are the more significant ones shared by research respondents.

- Adequate finances
- Health insurance, if health issues are involved
- Support from family and friends
- Pastoral support
- One or more people to talk with honestly and openly
- Support from a faith community
- Assistance in shouldering day-to-day responsibilities
- Ability to get away for rest and relaxation

The availability of these resources can affect how a person deals with a painful situation. Studies have shown that the more resources a person has, the better he or she is generally able to deal with crises or other difficulties.

The more you are able to understand a suffering individual and value him or her as a unique person with a unique life history, a unique set of circumstances, and a unique set of resources to draw on, the more likely you will be able to relate effectively with that person.

Come as a guest to the suffering person's house of pain—without assumptions, without judgment. Come with a heart open to understanding.

# 4

# WHO YOU BRING
# TO THE RELATIONSHIP

*Dear God, I wonder if I can do this. Can I really care for someone who is hurting? I know I can't do it alone. I need you. Prepare me. Be with me. Make me your tool. Most loving God, help me to sense the presence of Jesus at work in me and through me, so that the other person will see Jesus in me. And when I gaze into the eyes of the suffering one, help me to see the face of Jesus, so I always remember that as I care, I care for Jesus, and as I love, I love Jesus. Amen.*

Who you are is forever interwoven with what you do, whether in the arena of caregiving or any other in which you act. You are a tool that God has prepared for caring for others, and you carry that capacity within you all the time.

As a caregiver, you bring with you two most high and holy gifts to the one you care for. The correct question about these gifts is not, What are they? Rather, it is, *Who* are they?

The answer is basic: You bring Jesus, and you bring yourself.

That means Jesus incarnates himself in you, and when you bring yourself, you bring a complete package—your feelings, your wounds, and your presence—which gains its power because you have Jesus in you.

## INCARNATING THE COMPASSION OF CHRIST

Caregiving is not just a two-person relationship, but a three-person one. There's the one you care for, there's you, and there's Jesus. Jesus said, "Truly I tell you, just as you did it to one of the least of these who are members of my family, you did it to me" (Matthew 25:40 NRSV). Astonishing privilege! Jesus is already there ahead of you, in the one you care for, waiting for your care.

Nothing in you would make it possible for you to be worthy of this honor were it not for the fact that Jesus is also in you, working in you and reaching out through you. You communicate God to others in a language they can understand. It is the language of flesh and blood, the language of word and touch and, most especially, the language of ears—listening.

One woman knew intimately what it meant to have God's incarnational love present to her: "I remember the time I was in the hospital following cancer surgery. Late at night I got extremely cold and frightened. A nurse brought a warm blanket and then sat down beside me, calmly, gently stroking my hand. I was so thankful that I told her she was Jesus comforting me."

Relating to someone who is suffering at a deep level is a tremendously spiritual act. You meet the other person deeply, and you both meet God. Jesus is a powerfully active and present participant as you relate to that person.

The love you bring to suffering individuals is more than a mere reflection of God's love. It *is* God's love. First John 4:12 says that "if we love one another, God lives in us and his love is made complete in us." It isn't only your love that hurting people experience, but God's love in and through you. This is the love that has cherished them since before the foundations of the world. It is Love Incarnate who died and rose again for them in Jesus and dwells in them through the Spirit (Ephesians 1:3–14). And now, John says, this love is made complete for them through you.

Scary, wonderful, astonishing, humbling thought indeed!

Sometimes during prolonged suffering, people think that God has abandoned them. But if they can sense God's presence and love in you—a person they see, touch, and hear—they can take heart, knowing that God is near and will never leave them. Knowing this is priceless.

## YOU AND YOUR FEELINGS

Jesus is your greatest resource as you relate in a caring way to hurting people, and you yourself are your second greatest resource. You are an instrument of precision caring. True enough, you can learn certain skills and techniques that will enhance your helpfulness to another person, but all this is filtered through you—your genuine self, which you bring to the caring relationship.

### Like a Mother Hen

There is a beautiful New Testament Greek word, *proistanai,* which literally means "to stand in front of." The picture that makes the most sense of this word is of a mother hen guarding her brood by sheltering them under her wings. Perhaps you recall Jesus' lament for Jerusalem: "O Jerusalem, Jerusalem, you who kill the prophets and stone those sent to you, how often I have longed to gather your children together, as a hen gathers her chicks under her wings, but you were not willing" (Matthew 23:37).

This image Jesus uses is one way for you to think of your role in caring for those who are suffering. *Proistanai* describes a nurturing, shepherding kind of caring.

### Feelings: An Asset or a Liability?

The feelings you bring to the caregiving relationship can be both an asset and a liability. Your own array of feelings is what enables you to empathize with—to feel with—the one you are caring for. However, your feelings can also be an obstacle. If a suffering person's situation hits too close to home, you may get your own feelings mixed up with his or her feelings, and the caregiving boundaries may blur.

Feelings of anxiety and helplessness, common to everyone who relates to suffering people, may seem more like liabilities than assets. But anxiety can be a powerful motivator, a healthy impetus to get into action. On the other hand, if you feel overly anxious about a caregiving situation, you may be tempted to search for ways to make the other person feel better, to try and fix the other person. "You've got to be better so *I'm* more comfortable" was what one woman believed her caregivers were telling her.

## Caregiving Fears

People fear saying the wrong thing, blundering into the fragile self of the suffering person and making matters worse. No one wants to make a fool of him- or herself. No one wants to see a sufferer wince at what he or she has said.

Another fear is getting so close to another's hurt that you hurt too. Nobody enjoys taking on pain. The normal reaction is to avoid it. The stove is hot? Don't touch it, then. Avoidance is a healthy strategy in many situations of life, but not when relating to hurting individuals. It's not healthy for them, and it really isn't healthy for you, either.

Another fear, perhaps one that operates below the surface of conscious realization, is the fear of coming face-to-face with your own mortality. One woman called this the "fear of being dragged down as well."

It's all right to feel anxious. It's all right to feel helpless. Use those feelings as this man did: "When I admitted my anxiety and sense of helplessness to the sufferer, it broke the ice and made it clear that I was not some Superman there to save the day, but rather someone who would be there to help him ask the questions and express his feelings."

Even more, let anxious feelings be your signal to bring God into the picture, as another research participant suggests: "When I have these anxious or helpless feelings, the first thing I do is to pray. God has been my helper many times; he is my strength and helps me get through the rough times." Prayer is the antidote to the human tendency to concentrate on our own feelings instead of focusing on others.

Singing songs to a heavy heart can be an automatic reaction to suffering, like a music box wound up and set into motion. I see pain and suffering in front of me? I have to do something to make it go away. One person said it for all: "I have felt a powerful urge to try to give answers and fix the problem or try to relieve their pain. My struggle is to keep hands off and listen. I know now that I have selfishly tried to relieve my own anxieties about another's pain by trying to fix it and make it go away. This is me-centered, not other-centered."

Instead of resisting or denying your anxieties and feelings of helplessness, use them to help you relate more compassionately to those who are suffering. Give even these parts of yourself to God in prayer and ask him to use you, despite your fears and concerns. He will.

## THE WOUNDED CAREGIVER

The wounded caregiver is you. The term echoes the title of Henri Nouwen's book *The Wounded Healer,* and it involves embracing your own brokenness as you relate to those who suffer. Nouwen portrays the caring relationship as

> a deep human encounter in which a man is willing to put his own faith and doubt, his own hope and despair, his own light and darkness at the disposal of others who want to find a way through their confusion and touch the solid core of life.[1]

Compassion is the core element in caregiving, according to Nouwen:

> Through compassion it is possible to recognize that the craving for love that men feel resides also in our own hearts, that the cruelty that the world knows all too well is also rooted in our own impulses. Through compassion we also sense our hope for forgiveness in our friends' eyes and our hatred in their bitter mouths. When they kill, we know that we could have done it; when they give life, we know that we can do the same. For a compassionate man nothing human is alien: no joy and no sorrow, no way of living and no way of dying.[2]

And finally, Nouwen tells how compassion is central for your purposes in relating:

> The deeper [the compassionate one] is willing to enter into the painful condition which he and others know, the more likely it is that he can be a leader, leading his people out of the desert into the promised land.[3]

The desert Nouwen refers to is one the sufferer knows all too well, and Nouwen's point is that you, too, know it well. The depths of loneliness, fears, doubts, and pains—these are not alien to you. To the extent that you're in touch with those depths in yourself, to that same extent you will bring the most valuable quality of caring to the suffering individual.

The term *wounded caregiver* may conjure up images for you of searching your depths for experiences you have had that are similar to what the suffering person is experiencing. While such a search can sometimes be valid and worthwhile, it can also be a snare. You may wind up talking too much and listening too little, wrongly thinking that your experience can supply a shortcut for suffering people, a way of hurrying up their healing. One person put it this way: "If a caregiver has had a similar experience, this can be a blessing or a curse. It is a blessing if it causes the caregiver to remember what he or she would have wanted a caregiver to do. It's a curse if it causes the caregiver to focus the time telling the one who is suffering the nitty-gritties of this prior experience."

What you and the suffering person share is the human condition. Humans are more similar to one another than different. And Jesus has fully shared the human condition. This is the basis for *koinonia,* which is Christian fellowship at its deepest level.

## THE POWER OF PRESENCE

This chapter ends where it began, with the presence of Jesus. Over and over, research respondents reported presence alone as a powerful caring force. A woman who was 25 when her mother died said, "I don't remember anything they said, only their presence and prayers." Another said, "When people came and were just present for me, they were a gift. I felt love, compassion, and acceptance of the fact that I preferred silence over small talk. I was able to be lost in my own thoughts, yet not alone. They helped make a sad time a little more bearable."

This woman was describing the human presence of the one caring and relating. That's incarnation. Even when you don't mention the name of Jesus, he is still there in you, reaching out. One research participant said, "Their being with me helped me to remember that I'm never really alone, because God is always with me. A human presence makes God seem very near instead of far away."

When you don't know what to say, try saying nothing. Just let your quiet presence be the powerful witness to your love. Nouwen says it beautifully:

> If there is any posture that disturbs a suffering man or woman, it is aloofness. The tragedy of Christian ministry is that many who are in great need, many who seek an attentive ear, a word of support, a forgiving embrace, a firm hand, a tender smile, or even a stuttering confession of inability to do more, often find their ministers distant men who do not want to burn their fingers.[4]

Your presence is worth much, much more than words. Your presence communicates to the other that he or she is valued, precious, beloved. Your presence brings not only the gift of yourself into the relationship but also, in and through you, the gift of God.

# 5

# WHAT DO YOU DO
# AFTER YOU SAY HELLO?

*Dear God, I'm relying on you. Speak to me, and tell me what to say. Speak through me, and console the other. Speak for me, and tell the other what he or she needs to hear. Oh, and Lord—tell me when to be quiet, too. Thanks for being faithful. Amen.*

You've just heard that your friend has been diagnosed with a serious illness. You want to support your friend, but you can't imagine what you're going to say. Tempting as it is to avoid a visit, you know you can't allow yourself to do that. You call and make arrangements to see your friend.

You ring the bell and your friend opens the door. "Hello," you say.

"Hi. Come on in."

"Thanks," you say, and you step inside.

You are able to imagine the course of the conversation this far. But now here you are. What do you do or say next?

## CONNECTING MEANINGFULLY

Make your life simple. Here are some words almost magical in their effect: "It's good to see you." Just that.

You were maybe looking for something more profound? These words seem so simple, but they are profound in their effect. They have great power. They break the ice and connect you meaningfully with the other in an instant. Provided they're true, of course—that in your heart you truly find it "good to see" the other person.

So far, you've said, "Hello" and "It's good to see you." What's next?

Your next move may not be words at all. It could be touch. How much touch depends on your relationship with the other person and what both of you are comfortable with. You may do no more than reach out to touch the other person's arm or shoulder, or you may gather your friend into a warm hug.

So far, so good. You haven't sung any songs to the heavy-hearted one. You've greeted your friend, shared what is in your heart, and possibly touched him or her.

And if your friend still hasn't said anything? This isn't very likely because of how you have eased into the situation, but it could be so. More likely, the other individual has started to talk or maybe is shedding a tear. This is good. A great way to continue—and an almost surefire invitation to get the individual talking—is to say, "Fill me in on what's been going on." Other ways to say the same thing: "What's been happening?" or "Bring me up to date" or whatever other words you decide to use.

Maybe you've noticed that "How are you?" isn't included here. This question is not totally off-limits, but it often is not the best way to open a conversation, especially not the first time you visit with someone who is suffering. The immediate, unvoiced, internal response to *How are you?* could be *How do you think I am!*

Keep it simple.
"Hello."
"It's good to see you."
Possibly a touch.
"Fill me in on what's been happening."

Hurting people usually want to talk about their life situations. They will seize the opportunity to do so when given a chance. Your immediate goal is simply getting them to talk about what is concerning them right at that moment. That will be enough, if you allow it to happen. You don't have to think up perfect formula answers to questions. You don't have to theologize or psychologize or sing away the other's heavy heart. You couldn't do it anyway.

Sometime, probably earlier than later, it makes sense to say, "I'm sorry," or "I'm so sorry," or "I'm sorry that you are having to go through this." Sharing your sorrow is another powerful act. Your sorrow connects with the other's sorrow. For that moment, at least, you have stepped in to share the burden and lighten the load of the suffering individual.

One of the most effective and caring ways for you to invite the other person to open up is for you to do just the opposite. Be quiet. Listen! Listening much more than talking leads to success in caring.

## FOLLOW THE OTHER PERSON'S LEAD

Imagine this scenario. A friend's mother has just died at the age of 85. She had lived a full and vibrant life for 80 of those years but in the last 5 has been declining steadily. Your friend has just told you the news. What do you say?

You may be tempted to say, "Well, she lived a full life," or "It's for the best." But wait for your friend to suggest such a conclusion. When someone said, "He lived a good life," to one woman upon the death of her 81-year-old father, her response was an indignant "How dare you! You don't understand at all—he is my father!'"

Follow the other person's lead. What is your best response to the news of a very sick or very old person's death? Say, "I'm sorry to hear that," and wait for your friend to indicate how he or she feels about the situation. Your friend may very well say, "It's for the best," or "My mother lived a long and good life," and then you could agree. You might even open the door to further sharing of feelings by saying, "I suppose so, but I would imagine it still hurts."

While your friend may very well be glad that the loved one's suffering is over, at the same time he or she has lost someone dear. In many instances, a bereaved person experiences mixed feelings. Even if your friend is likely to say that the death was for the best, it is most caring to allow him or her to say so first. If you jump in with such a comment, you actually might delay or prevent his or her coming to that realization.

Play it safe. Initially, simply express your sorrow. Follow the other person's lead from there on.

What does it mean to follow the other person's lead? Do a lot of listening to understand his or her mind and heart. Someone who is grieving or in pain typically has conflicting feelings and thoughts that shift, sometimes back and forth in the same hour—even in the same minute! Your focused listening puts you in tune with that person. He or she realizes that you truly understand, which makes your presence all the more healing to the one with a heavy heart.

Letting the other person take the lead is a way for you to show that you value and prize that individual. Letting him or her lead is also an act of humility. You acknowledge that you don't know it all.

## FOCUS ON THE OTHER PERSON

Remember from the beginning that your conversation with a suffering person is not about "us"—meaning not about you *and* the other person, as conversations usually flow. It is strictly about the one who is suffering. This conversation is between unequals because, at that moment, one person has a heavier load to carry than the other.

Go into such interactions forgetting about yourself and your own needs. Easy to say, hard to do. Such a completely other-focused way of being—way of loving!—is so rare that it has its own name: *agape love.* Other-focused and unconditional love is what God has for us humans, and we struggle to follow Jesus' example and offer it to others. This struggle is worthwhile, however. The more you are able to focus on the other person, the better friend, relative, neighbor, work associate, or significant other you will be to that suffering person.

How do you know when you're straying from concern for the other to a focus on yourself? Several sentence starters can send out warning signals. If your natural response to your friend's pain is to use any of these sentence starters, you *may be* shifting the focus to yourself.

- "Well, I . . ."
- "When I . . ."
- "I remember . . ."
- "My . . ."

In these instances and many others, the caregiver interjects his or her memories and experiences, removing the focus from the suffering individual. Instead of shining the soft light of love on the other person, the speaker shifts the spotlight to him- or herself.

It is very natural, very human, to focus on yourself. An old joke reveals this habit at work: "But that's enough about me," said the bore. "What do *you* think about me?" Laughter at this joke is rueful at best. While we all recognize the exaggeration in that persona, deep down we worry that it might be more true of us than we like to think.

Conversations with a suffering person call us to set aside our own thoughts and needs and focus completely on the other's needs. Because we are human, we will not achieve the perfect, unconditional, other-centered love that God manages—but we can move closer to it.

## Sharing Personal Experiences

In our war with her cancer, Joan and I related to a multitude of medical personnel—physicians, nurses, technicians, and others. There were a few times when they shared their own experiences with cancer. Once, when Joan was facing a particular medical test and was quite fearful, she asked the oncology research nurse if the procedure were as painful as getting a shot of a particular blood enhancer. The nurse responded that it would not be as painful as the shot, and then she added, "I've had both." Those few words confirmed her own personal experience with cancer and made both of us feel more at ease.

Before another medical procedure, Joan was expressing quite a bit of anxiety. The nursing supervisor came right out and told us that she was a breast cancer survivor, had gone through this test, and knew that, while it was uncomfortable, it was very tolerable. Before us, we knew, was a fellow sojourner, and that was very encouraging.

Another instance meant a lot to me as someone supporting a family member with cancer. At one point we had been working with a particular oncologist for four months and probably had contact with her 20 to 30 times, both in her office and in the hospital. One evening I was with Joan as she underwent a particularly difficult and painful test. The oncologist asked to speak with me privately to schedule an appointment for the next morning. During the conversation she said, "I know this is very difficult for you. I've been there myself." I asked her, "Have you had a loved one who has had cancer?" She said, "Yes, I have, which is why I know it is very difficult." At that point I just about melted, feeling so good that this physician was sharing this fact about her life with me.

Sharing personal experiences with those who are hurting can be tricky. Here are some guidelines that can affect how well your personal example might be received by another person.

1. Use personal experiences sparingly. The danger is always that you will shift the focus away from the suffering individual.

2. Share personal examples later rather than sooner. Over and over, research respondents said how much they appreciated individuals' sharing personal experiences when the sharing was accompanied by a good amount of listening both before and after they shared their personal experiences. Sharing personal experiences becomes less helpful when you make them one-way communications with your story as the centerpiece.

3. Be brief. You don't need to relay every aspect of your experience. You may be tempted to share more detail than necessary. There is one excellent way to determine if more is called for: Allow the person to ask for more information. Once again, you will want to carefully follow his or her lead.

4. Sharing how you handled a painful situation can either be helpful or harmful to a hurting individual. If you present yourself as an imperfect human being, struggling with and working through a particular issue or situation, your story may be comforting. But if you imply that you handled the event in an almost superhuman or saintlike fashion, your story may seem judgmental to the suffering individual.

5. Avoid telling a suffering person about a traumatic, painful, or difficult experience that you have endured. For example, sharing the saga of your own anguished deliveries with a nervous, first-time mother who is soon to give birth is thoughtless and unkind. Consider how your story might affect the distressed person before you decide to share it.

6. If you have been through an experience similar to the one an individual is facing, you could share information that would relieve his or her anxiety or otherwise help him or her to face this experience. You may also know of a particular support group tailored to the kind of suffering the other person is going through. You might know of a treatment, a counselor, a physician, a clinic—factual information from personal experience that would make life easier for the individual.

Sharing your personal experience can communicate a powerful message: "You are not alone." Your personal story may also communicate hope to the other person. Just be careful not to shift the focus away from the suffering individual.

## SHARING THE EXPERIENCES OF OTHERS

What about sharing the experiences of others? This is even trickier than sharing your own experiences of pain and suffering. All the cautions about sharing personal experiences apply—only much more so.

One reflective research participant noted that "whether to share stories of others depends. One person could share such a story, and you would feel like you were not alone in your own struggle. Then it can be a source of comfort and hope. But sometimes the person sharing can seem to be saying, 'Well, this person went through this or worse and he or she is doing fine, so what is your problem?'"

Others commented that they could not even think about the pain others had experienced because they were consumed or overwhelmed by their own pain and suffering. "You don't need any comparisons when you are in pain," another person noted. "Your pain is *yours,* and all you want to deal with is *your* pain. You are in a tunnel—all alone— you want someone just to be there with you." Telling an individual about the experiences of others often makes that person feel more alone because the focus is no longer on him or her but on another person's story.

There is one kind of story that should *never* be shared— horror stories! What strange impulse compels people to respond to the news of another's suffering with, "Oh yeah, my uncle had that—and he died" or some variation thereof? From job loss to illness, there seems to be a horror story to match or exceed every situation. At the very least, horror stories do a disservice to the one in pain by implying that such horrible exceptions are the norm or that the outcome is already determined. The suffering person you are relating to has enough to contend with already and doesn't need you to add the weight of despair to an already heavy heart.

Sharing experiences of others with someone in pain is usually not a caring practice. It separates a sufferer by one more degree from the relevance of what you are sharing. The person in pain wants to know that you are hearing and empathizing with him or her "up close and personal," not from the detached and safe distance of someone else's suffering.

Most research participants and reviewers were adamant in their counsel that caregivers should almost always avoid sharing the experiences of others with those who are suffering. One person gave this wise advice: "Others' stories can help in sermons, testimonies, and classes, but in one-to-one sharing the only important story is the one of the person experiencing the pain at the time."

## WHAT DO YOU DO WHEN THERE'S NOTHING TO SAY?

Sometimes silence fills the room where you and the suffering person are. What do you do?

Most of us feel very uncomfortable with silence. When caregivers were asked what they do in situations of silence, many indicated their discomfort: "Try to overcome my own anxiety"; "Try to be comfortable with silence"; or "I'm learning that silence is okay. I'm still not 100% comfortable with it, but I'm learning that sometimes it's a good thing."

Silence can mean different things. Perhaps the suffering person is simply overwhelmed with feelings and needs to be still for a while.

Another possibility is that the person may be processing what has gone before. This takes time. You need the patience to simply be there and let the individual know by your presence and gentle words that, when and if he or she wants to talk, you're willing to listen. One man reported that he quietly tells the silent person, "I don't know what to say or do right now, so I'll just be here with you if that's OK."

Sometimes, silence results from the hurting person's not knowing how to receive the care you are offering. One woman described what she learned as a care receiver about silence: "I think for me it was a process of learning to accept care from people who were very patient with me during times of silence. Sometimes, they could see into my pain so clearly when I couldn't verbalize it, and they just allowed me to feel what I felt. As I look back, they held my silence as much as my pain."

You don't need to be totally passive during such a silence, not by any means. Touch the suffering individual—hold the person's hands, pat a shoulder, give a hug—whatever is appropriate. Cry together. Most importantly, you can use the quiet to pray silently for the hurting person and to ask for guidance in your caring. A perceptive pastor shared that he often prays these words: "O Lord, please keep your arm around my shoulder and your hand over my mouth."

When silence fills the room, remember that God is beneath and within the silence, radiating his love. You are always there as God's emissary of love. You can speak in love, you can listen in love, and you can simply be with the other person in love.

# 6

# CRY, FEEL AWFUL

*Dear God, sometimes I feel uncomfortable when some-
one cries in front of me. I know you've provided tears for
times when words aren't adequate to express the depths
of pain and suffering. Jesus wept. Teach me to embrace
the tears of those who are hurting and at times even to
weep with them. Amen.*

In March 1993 the University of Michigan played the
University of North Carolina for the NCAA basketball
championship. Michigan had a particularly good team that
year and was favored to win. They didn't. The University of
North Carolina played an excellent game, and right at the
end of the game, Michigan made a costly mistake that
caused them to lose the game.

With the University of Michigan team already in its
locker room, the Michigan coach, Steve Fisher, was interviewed briefly just outside the locker-room door. One of the
sports reporters asked Coach Fisher, "What are you going to
tell your team?"

Coach Fisher replied, "Cry, feel awful."

On the surface this seems like a very uncoachlike thing to say. Shouldn't a coach be saying to players, "We'll win next year," or "You can be proud of yourselves, you played a good game," or "We did well even to get this far." But there was brilliance in what Steve Fisher said. The brilliance lay in a coach who was helping his players to feel first things first, to acknowledge that they felt terrible to have come this far and then to have lost. What a way to clear out their emotions so that team members could get on with their lives.

## A GOOD CRY

Sometimes people just need to cry.

Tears are cleansing. Denying tears to hurting individuals can prevent them from working through and cleaning out their pain right at the most appropriate and beneficial time for this cleansing.

Someone told a research participant whose spouse had died, "Don't cry—you'll make yourself sick." Wrong! Crying is healing. It releases tension and gets painful feelings out in the open.

There is often a heavy price to pay for not crying. Burying feelings—pretending that all is well, keeping a stiff upper lip—is a very real danger to one's emotional, psychological, spiritual, and physical self. Pressuring someone to bury feelings sets up that individual for a crash later. The crash may show itself in depression and in prolonged suffering and grief.

You can play a significant part in another's life if you accept that it is perfectly all right for that individual to cry— even better, if you accept that crying is part of healing. Caregivers sometimes worry that if a suffering person breaks into tears, it must mean that the caregiver has done something wrong. In truth, most of the time it means just the opposite—you've done something right, very right. People cry in front of those they feel safe with, those they trust. If a hurting person cries in your presence, you are trusted.

## "Thanks for Believing Me"

During one prolonged hospital stay, Joan had tubes going in and coming out every which way, keeping her from moving around much. She described to me how she was feeling—miserable, frustrated, and depressed. I listened and said to her, "I know."

She looked me right in the eyes and said, "Thanks for believing me."

I wasn't saying that I totally understood how she was feeling, but I knew she was telling the truth as she described her feelings.

When a suffering individual describes how he or she feels, believe what you hear and communicate your belief. You are not that person. You can't truly feel what he or she feels. But you can refrain from disbelieving or trying to talk that person out of his or her feelings.

When suffering people realize that you are hearing and believing them, they experience great comfort. Your simple act of validating a person's feelings can help that individual not to feel so alone. In recognizing the pain or discomfort he or she is feeling, you become a partner with that person. You communicate that you share in his or her world. You warm the person's heart.

One person put it like this: "It was extremely important that people believed that my pain was real, rather than telling me not to feel it or invalidating it in some way." The issue is not even what anyone else, or most everyone else, would feel. The only issue is what that person in front of you feels.

In the days between the time that Joan was tentatively diagnosed with ovarian cancer and the surgery confirming that diagnosis, we gave considerable attention to the post-surgical treatment that she might receive, including chemotherapy. Chemotherapy would likely cause hair loss, which greatly distressed Joan. We read some literature and talked to a resource person who shared information about various types of wigs, so we knew what options were available. But Joan simply was not at all happy at the prospect of losing her hair.

Joan's surgery took place early on a Friday morning. A nurse told several of us who had been with Joan through the night that this would be a good time for us to get some breakfast in the hospital cafeteria because she would be in surgery for several hours.

At breakfast the subject turned to how we could help Joan cope with the reality of her impending hair loss. The discussion ranged from telling Joan how natural wigs looked to the fact that she should be thankful that hair loss was one side effect of chemotherapy that would not require additional medication to manage.

About that time, a woman who worked for Joan's oncologist stopped by our table to greet us. She was a cancer survivor herself and had lost her hair twice. Someone at the table asked her what would be the best thing to say to Joan to help her accept losing her hair and recognize the benefits of getting a good wig.

The woman paused briefly and then said with conviction, "I'd tell her I wouldn't want to lose my hair either."

What powerful words! They immediately moved the conversation from trying to convince Joan that losing her hair was no big deal to acknowledging her distress over the prospect of losing an important part of what defined her.

What can you say when a hurting individual tells you, "I don't want to do that"—carry through on a difficult decision, take a painful medical test, whatever the painful situation is? A validating response is, "Of course you don't." If appropriate, you might add, "I wouldn't either." With those words, you are validating the person's pain and discomfort. He or she has suddenly gained a soul mate in you, one who understands how difficult the situation is and affirms his or her feelings.

You might be concerned that in saying these words you are aiding and abetting the individual to avoid something necessary. Not at all. You aren't saying, "I don't think you should do that." Rather, you are telling the individual that you understand how difficult it is. This response not only communicates that the hurting individual has a soul mate, but it also builds your credibility for possibly talking with that person later about following through with what needs to be done.

Most importantly, your understanding keeps the other from digging in and establishing a defensive position. You've certainly seen that kind of behavior—or perhaps engaged in it yourself. Someone advances all kinds of rational reasons why thus-and-so is a wise course of action, and the immediate reaction is to argue and harden in opposition.

In truth, validating someone's feelings often frees that person to decide for him- or herself to go ahead and do whatever needs to be done. Validating feelings actually encourages and empowers good decision making.

## Sharing the Hurt

Scripture blesses the notion of sharing the hurt with those who are suffering. "Remember those in prison as if you were their fellow prisoners, and those who are mistreated as if you yourselves were suffering" (Hebrews 13:3). This is an invitation to empathy, joining your feelings with the feelings of another *as if* you yourself were experiencing them.

But Scripture pushes for an even greater commingling of your feelings with those of the sufferer: "Rejoice with those who rejoice, weep with those who weep" (Romans 12:15 NRSV). This passage invites us to cast aside our emotional reservations and to cry with the one who is weeping. The Greek word for *weep* used in this verse, as well as several other New Testament passages, is a demonstrative word. It does not mean to cry silently, but to sob or wail loudly. It is an obvious display of grief.

If you are well acquainted with the hurting person, one of the most powerfully caring acts you can do—when you genuinely feel it—is to share the hurt. You can do this by putting your hand on the person's shoulder or giving him or her a hug. You can join in tears with the person, feeling bad and suffering right along with him or her. Caution: Do not take this so far that the suffering person suddenly feels obliged to become a caregiver for you. You aren't trying to reverse roles here. Your tears are simply telling the other person that you are feeling his or her pain, too.

If you feel terrible about the situation, you don't need to cover that up. You can say, "I feel terrible, too," when the other tells you that's how he or she feels. Just saying words like these can lift a suffering person's spirits. The hurting person often feels a warm glow inside when he or she realizes that someone else is hurting alongside. Here's how one woman described that feeling.

> Our pastor lost his son in a terrible accident with a loaded gun. All of us in the church were devastated by it and mourned with him. A few years later we lost our son, and our pastor reached out to us. His hugs and warm touches and tears—we just looked at each other, and I knew what he was thinking and he knew what I was thinking. There is nothing better than the warmth of a shared connection with somebody who is hurting right along with you.

People too commonly try giving pep talks when others are in pain. It doesn't work. What does? Sharing the pain on a deep level. One of the apocryphal books says, "Do not avoid those who weep, but mourn with those who mourn" (Sirach 7:34 NRSV). This wise statement shows clear knowledge of one human tendancy: People are tempted to avoid those who are weeping. The writer of Sirach adds emphasis to Romans 12:15. Don't avoid those who are mourning. Instead, reach out to them, embrace their weeping, and weep right along with them if that's natural and appropriate both for you and the situation.

In other words, share the hurt.

## HAVING IT OUT WITH GOD

Does God want to have a relationship with the real you? Or will God be content to have a relationship with some phony, prettied-up, pious you?

This question is posed in such a way that you can't get the answer wrong. God wants the real me, you say. Of course!

If you accept that, then the next question is, *How angry are you allowed to get at God?* How much wailing, screaming, crying, and venting are you allowed?

*As much as it takes* is the answer. *As much as your feelings demand.*

The truth about God here is very clear: God can take whatever you can dish out. In the same way, God can handle whatever the suffering person dishes out. It's inappropriate for you to quiet someone who is ranting angrily at God: "Hush, hush. You know you don't mean that." It's a great temptation to stifle the other person's anger or grief-stricken sobs or questioning of God, to try to defend God—who doesn't need defending.

Like Job's friends, some people think that when a suffering person lashes out at God, his or her anger reflects a weak faith. After all, they reason, who are we to question God about anything that happens to us?

I really like what Philip Yancey says about relating honestly to God: "One bold message in the Book of Job is that you can say anything to God. Throw at him your grief, your anger, your doubt, your bitterness, your betrayal, your disappointment—he can absorb them all."[1]

It seems so disrespectful, if not downright dangerous, to rail at God, you might think. A quick glance at the Psalms shows that those who wrote them did just that, pleading with God to listen to them, wondering why God seemed so far away in their times of trouble. Psalm 22 shows the full progression that takes place when someone is allowed to express his or her feelings. "My God, my God, why have you forsaken me!" the psalmist cries in the first verse. By the end of the psalm he has calmed down and realizes that he can rely on God and extol God to others in a stronger-than-ever expression of faith. But it took time—and a lot of weeping, wailing, and questioning—to reach that point.

One pastor described his own experience struggling with God: "I think God-wrestling is essential to journeying through pain and suffering. I had people around me who kept showing me tangible, real, felt acts of a faithful, trustworthy God. Because of their faith holding me up, I was free to struggle, wrestle, fight, and, finally, make peace with God."

*Trustworthy God* is the key term in that pastor's statement. Trusting God is what it's all about. Strongly questioning God isn't evidence of a lack of faith or even of the lack of a relationship with God. Rather, those who question

God, especially those who question him strongly, are by this very act showing that they trust God deeply enough to risk questioning him.

The foundation of that kind of relationship is love. People don't question or rail at someone they don't care about. If someone is striking out at God, get out of the way and let the person have his or her say. Better yet, don't get out of the way. Walk with the person.

Don't worry about the faith of those in the midst of life's trials who are furiously struggling with God. They are in God's hands as they struggle. As they beat against God's chest, God's loving arms are waiting to enfold them.

Your job is to be Jesus right then and there to them. Because you are the embodiment of God, Jesus in the flesh to that person, he or she is by no means alone and separated from God as the struggle goes on. When suffering people are pushing away from God, let them push! The harder they push, the more likely they will experience the depth of God's compassion and the certainty of God's presence.

## The Closest Thing to a Magic Bullet

Listening is the closest thing to a magic bullet you will find in your kit of caring skills. You might try setting yourself a radical goal of doing nothing more than listening in a caring visit. You won't be able to manage 100% listening, but setting your goal high means you will listen much more than you talk.

Some research participants told how listening made a difference for them in their pain:

- "My brother died from a drug overdose. A few let me tell the story over and over. They let me be sad without trying to change me."
- "When I was divorced, a close friend was an excellent listener. He was there for me whenever I needed him and did not offer any simple answers or pat advice."
- "After infertility treatments, I lost my twins at 21 weeks. A woman from church whom I knew only casually called and shared that she had lost a child at 34 weeks. She came over to my house and just sat with me—just sat and listened and cried with me. That was irreplaceable."
- "My friends asked me to do the things with them I had always done, and they were willing to stop and listen to my pain whenever and wherever it came out."
- "When one of my parents died, the ones who helped me were the ones who said little."

When you listen, you are concentrating on the other. The force of this concentration is healing in and of itself. You allow the suffering individual to vent, if that's what the person needs to do. You gain a reputation for being wise and full of insight simply by allowing the other to learn from hearing him- or herself talk. Job's counselors, his friends, didn't get into trouble until they started to talk. According to Job 2:13, they sat with him for seven days and seven nights and didn't say a word to him. Up to that point, they looked like geniuses. It wasn't until they opened their mouths that the illusion was shattered.

Those who are suffering need the kind of friend Terri Green describes: "Being a listening friend is like being someone's human journal. The journal . . . accepts every word that you write, unconditionally. A journal gives you the opportunity to vent without being criticized."[2]

Listening is a caregiving skill that is readily available but, at the same time, so elusive. Sometimes caregivers simply feel anxious around suffering individuals and because of their anxiety end up talking more than they ordinarily would. Also, many caregivers don't think they have accomplished anything until they have shared some words of wisdom with someone who is suffering.

The very best gift you can offer a suffering person is a heart full of understanding, eyes filled with tears, and ears ready to listen.

# 7

# WISHING HURTS AWAY—
# DON'T YOU WISH!

*Listen, Lord: With your muscle and my brains, we can fix this situation. . . . Oh? You'd rather use my muscle and your brains? You think loving care will work here? Well, I guess you know what you're doing, Lord. But I'm ready to consult with you anytime you want suggestions. . . . Amen.*

At times it can seem so easy for you to see. You have such a clear picture of what a hurting person should be thinking, feeling, and doing. You are certain that the suffering person needs to move from point A to point B as quickly as possible. You just have to help the other person find the way.

If only you could take the pain away! You want to help so badly. So do I. But this strong desire to help the other person—which motivates us tremendously in our caring—sometimes gets in the way of our relating effectively.

Consider some of the goals you might want to achieve as you relate to someone who is suffering. You might want to help the person—

1. Get better

2. Accept his or her situation

3. See the hopeful side of the situation

4. Make healthy choices

5. Maintain good relations with relatives and friends

6. Feel close to God

7. Develop stronger faith

8. Inspire others by his or her Christian response to pain and suffering

These are great goals, no doubt about it. You probably wouldn't get much argument from those who are suffering—they want these outcomes, too. But suffering people almost never arrive at one of these desired outcomes as a result of another person's mapping out a particular path for them. They will not achieve these attitudes and behaviors by setting them as goals and striving to reach them, nor will they reach them faster as a result of anyone's prodding. It simply doesn't work that way.

In fact, the best way to ensure that suffering people *don't* arrive at the emotional and spiritual place you both desire is to impose your thoughts, feelings, or beliefs on them in an attempt to help them feel better or "get over it."

So what does work and what really helps suffering people? Your being fully present to them and allowing God to heal while you care. Many caregivers find this to be a tremendously freeing truth, as did one caregiver who participated in the research: "When I first realized that I didn't have to provide all the answers or solve the problems in my caregiving, it was like a huge weight being lifted from me."

Following are some natural human tendencies that can block effective caring. Each in its own way is an attempt to move the hurting person along a prescribed path instead of meeting the person in the moment and walking where he or she leads.

## THE HUMAN DESIRE TO WANT TO FIX THINGS

Suppose you were getting your house ready for sale. A leak in the roof has stained one of the walls. You can cover the stain with wallpaper long enough to sell the house and get out of town, leaving the new buyer to deal with the next rainstorm. Or you can take the more costly approach and repair the roof, then paint or wallpaper over the stain.

When you relate to a hurting person, you can choose the cheap and easy approach, papering over the other person's pain. Or you can choose the costly approach, listening to find out what the person's real problems are and being there for him or her in the thick of those real problems.

A man who had been fired from his dream job reported: "I heard the clichés everyone knows. Some people were more interested in 'fixing' me instead of letting me work through my grief and feelings of failure. It was hard for me to accept these cliché people, although sometimes I could tell they just didn't know what to say."

A desire to "make it all better" usually arises from the best of intentions. The trouble is that when you try to fix someone else's emotional or spiritual problem quickly you usually just cover up his or her pain. An insightful research participant explains: "The tendency to fix things overlooks feelings. It bypasses where the person actually is at the moment and attempts to put healing in the hands of the caregiver."

Suffering people do not respond well to quick fixes or easy solutions because this approach short-circuits the normal coping process. As one woman said, "If we attempt to fix someone's problems, we've taken away that person's chance to learn or improve their coping skills. Although we may want the person to get better quickly, it is not our function to go in and do it ourselves!"

Another man wrote, "This has been a very difficult issue for me. I always have to be careful not to put on my 'Mr. Fix-it' hat. I tend to be outcome-driven, and that can very easily spill over to my role as a caregiver. When I hear about a problem causing suffering, I naturally want to get in there and see what I can do to try to fix things. This is a tendency that I must consciously watch and avoid."

"It seems easier to give advice or to 'help' by trying to change the situation than to let ourselves be uncomfortable with someone else's pain or suffering," agreed one caregiver. Another remarked, "I have to learn to 'be with' and not 'act for' the person I'm caring for." Still another caregiver added, "It's the difference between quietly sitting with them while they mourn versus quickly trying to find a way to dry their eyes."

Wanting to fix things—and fix things right away—does not make you bad. It makes you human. Recognizing this very human tendency can give you a tremendous head start in managing it. Rather than trying the quick and easy fix, you instead create the time and space for the other person to work through the healing process.

Fixing can be okay, as long as it's dinner or the other person's car. But trying to fix a person is not an appropriate or even attainable goal. Here's a good rule of thumb: *Fix things; relate to people.*

## PRESET AGENDAS

Planning ahead of time how your interaction with a hurting person ought to go is very unproductive. In a desire to be helpful, you plan just where you want the conversation to go, and then you set about trying to make that happen during the interaction.

As well-meaning as this outcome-based plan might be, it seldom works, and it can get in the way of real relating. If you are acting like a border collie, trying to herd someone this way and that in an attempt to get to your goal, the person will know it. He or she will either resist your directions or silently go along without owning the process and without being helped by it.

One of the problems with a preplanned agenda is that you may be so focused on maneuvering the other person that you aren't attentive to his or her needs. Henri Nouwen wrote, "So we find it extremely hard to pay attention because of our intentions. As soon as our intentions take over, the question no longer is, 'Who is he?' but, 'What can I get from him?'—

and then we no longer listen to what he is saying but to what we can do with what he is saying."[1]

You might imagine that you would never relate to a hurting person with the notion of "What can I get from this person?" And yet . . . sometimes what I want, even though I may have trouble identifying it beneath the jumble of my motives and desires to help, is nothing more complicated than relief from my own discomfort. It might be so with you too. You might have difficulty facing another person's pain. If you look below the surface, you might find that you also want to smooth things over for your own sake.

Your best agenda is *not* to have an agenda—except to follow the agenda of the suffering person. When you do that, you are really caring.

## HITTING HOME RUNS

You don't have to "hit a home run" in your interactions with suffering individuals, to say or do exactly the right thing to make the person feel completely better immediately. The truth is, in most situations of significant struggle and suffering, nothing you can say or do will make the pain go away. The suffering person doesn't need a home run hitter; he or she needs your consistent, caring presence.

This point is not, "Don't hit home runs." It is rather, "Don't *try* to hit home runs." The baseball player who swings for the fences is less likely to hit a home run than the one who takes a smooth, level swing at a good pitch. If you try to hit every pitch over the outfield wall, most of the time you'll just strike out.

Sudden breakthroughs do occur in caring relationships, but they are few and far between—and they are not the result of careful strategizing. While strategizing is essential in many task-oriented areas of life, when you're relating to someone who is suffering, such planning hurts much more than it helps. Instead, taking the faithful, consistent approach to caring means the pressure is off. You are not expected or required to hit a home run. The more you release yourself from that expectation, the more effective you will be in caring for others.

Hurts don't go away because you wish them away or reason them away. In fact, *nothing* you as a caregiver can do will miraculously remove the pain. That's God's terrain. So don't expect that you will be able to provide just what the person needs to make it all better. You have been called to fulfill a role that is much more attainable—walking with the person, sharing and being Christ's love and compassion. When you do that, you will be making a significant difference in the suffering person's life.

# 8

# FOR BETTER OR FOR WORSE

*Dear God, tune me in to you, and to the needs of the suffering one. Help me to balance on this tightrope of not-too-much-too-soon and not-too-little-too-late. Enable me to reach out with your love and be as consistent in my caring as you are in caring for me. In Jesus' name. Amen.*

Caring is action, not just good intentions. Caring occurs when you express your good intentions through loving—and appropriate—deeds. As someone wanting to be God's love to suffering persons, you will be more or less helpful in your care for such individuals depending on what you do. Fulfill caring actions effectively, and they bring hope and encouragement to the sufferer. Do them less effectively, and they may not be everything you had wanted them to be.

Feedback from research participants who had received care shaped the guidelines for the six caring actions covered in this chapter. These practical principles are not meant to inhibit you, rather to free you to care most effectively.

Absorb them, assimilate them, and then go and care!

## SENDING CARDS AND NOTES

People almost always appreciate receiving a card or note. A written communication is far less invasive than a ringing telephone, and they can save it to read more than once. Here are three principles to maximize the caring potential of cards and notes.

### *Write a Personal Note*

Sending a card is good. Adding a personal paragraph or two is great. Research participants consistently reported that, while they appreciated receiving cards with just a signature or a one-line comment on them, they preferred:

- Store-bought cards with one or more paragraphs written on them by the sender
- Cards with a separate note included
- Blank cards with a handwritten note inside
- Notes on stationery

Research respondents frequently mentioned that they often saved cards with notes added to reread later. Their comfort lasts.

### *Focus on the Suffering Person*

The *first time* you send a note or card to someone experiencing a significant crisis, focus totally on the suffering person and his or her pain. This is not the occasion to share newsy tidbits or stories about yourself or your family. Chances are good that the suffering person won't feel very cared for if your card or note reads something like this: "I heard you are getting a divorce, and I am very sorry to hear that. Our news is that David made the varsity basketball team and . . . and . . . and . . ."

A helpful message will be sprinkled with *you*s and *your*s as in the following:

- "I'm sorry to hear about *your* . . ."
- *"You* have been on my mind a lot lately."
- "This must be so difficult for *you.*"
- "It hurts to know that *you* are going through this."
- "Our hearts go out to *you.*"
- "_____ told me about *your* setback."

Subsequent communications may include personal news when appropriate, but as long as the person's suffering continues, be sure to focus much of your writing on the hurting individual.

Think *you* as you write.

### *Write Your Heart*

As you think about filling some of that space on a card or piece of stationery, imagine the other person is right there in front of you. What can you say to communicate your deep concern? Write with your heart, not just your head. Don't hold back. Pour out your emotions on the card or paper in front of you. Here are examples of what people have written to hurting individuals:

- "I know you are hurting, and I wish I could be there."
- "We are deeply saddened by the news of . . ."
- "My heart broke when I heard that . . ."

- "The news of your suffering knocked the breath out of us."
- "I wish I could take the pain away."

Let your message spontaneously express how you feel inside as you think about the suffering person.

## MAKING PHONE CALLS

To telephone or not to telephone is often the question. Maybe you've been in the middle of a crisis and found a ringing telephone only added to the chaos of your life. At other times, the sound of a friendly voice has been a comfort. If you are not sure how a phone call would be received, a better choice might be to put down the telephone and pick up a pen. Here are a few ways to make your calls as effective—and welcome—as possible.

### *The Closer Your Relationship, the Freer You Can Be to Telephone*

How close you are to a person enhances your sensitivity to his or her needs. Be more cautious about calling if you don't know the person well. One woman, whose husband had been in the hospital and still required a good deal of care after his release, shared this: "I was quite busy. I had to do a lot of things for his care. I didn't need a lot of phone calls right at that point. There were family members and others close to us I had to talk to, to keep them up-to-date. I would just as soon others had written."

Another woman, speaking of the death of her brother, said, "From people who were *not* close to me, I appreciated written communications more. When my brother died, I was just too emotional to speak with people other than those who were close to me."

These comments also suggest a caring action you may offer, if appropriate, to someone who is suffering: screening phone calls or returning answering machine messages. One woman indicated why a friend's handling her phone calls meant so much to her: "I got overwhelmed sometimes with so many people calling. I just plain got tired of telling the same story over and over and over again and was glad someone could do that for me."

Find out if this is a service that the hurting person would like for you to handle and when such help would be the most welcome. He or she could identify any callers that require personal calls and tell you what to say. You might say something like this: "Hello, this is Betty Smith. Jane Davis has asked me to get back to all of the people who have been calling to thank you for your expressions of concern and support. So many people have been calling that Jane can't return all the calls because she's spending most of her time caring for Harold. Jane asked me to update you on Harold's situation. *[Share the information that Jane gave you.]* Is there any message you want me to give to Jane? *[Write down the message.]* Jane wants me to pass on her appreciation for your support and prayers. She looks forward to talking with you personally when things settle down."

### Gauge the Time to Call

Making a phone call to someone who is ill or in the midst of a painful situation raises a lot of questions. What is the person's schedule? How is the person feeling? How many times has the phone rung already? Is the person napping?

The more you know about the person's situation, the better you'll know the best time to call. For example, if the individual needs a lot of rest, don't call at times when he or she is likely to be sleeping. As a general rule, call when other family members will probably be there, so the suffering person won't be disturbed.

In the earliest stages of someone's suffering, phone calls and visits are both likely to be plentiful. Keep your initial call brief—long enough to express your genuine concern, but not so long as to tie up the phone line when close family members or helping professionals may need to reach the person.

Another question is what kind of message to leave on an answering machine. After an initial greeting, you might say, "I just wanted to let you know that I'm really sorry about *[whatever the situation is]*. No need to call me back. I'll get in touch with you later." The key part of this message is *no need to call me back.*

One woman whose husband was in the hospital for 31 days said, "I found the phone calls disrupting to me, over-whelming. I was at the hospital all day, and when I'd come home at night, I was exhausted. I still had to let my children or out-of-state family know what was going on—but there also would be ten messages on my answering machine."

Letting suffering individuals know that you are thinking of or praying for them can be a comfort. Assuring them that you do not expect a return call lifts an additional burden from them.

### *Ask Whether It's a Good Time to Talk*

Even if you plan your call for the most opportune time, you may still reach the other person when he or she is not able to talk. The best way to determine whether your call is welcome is to ask, "Is this a good time?" Give the person permission to say, "No, this is not a particularly good time." Then graciously and quickly say your farewell.

Some suffering people may feel obliged to talk even if they would rather not. Listen for verbal cues to tell you if the person really can't or doesn't want to talk right then. If this seems to be the case, just speak briefly with the person before wrapping up the phone call. If, however, the person sounds genuinely available and eager to talk, enjoy the conversation.

### *Don't* **Talk** *on the Telephone;* **Listen** *on the Telephone*

People making a phone call sometimes worry needlessly about what they should say. The good news is that you don't need to say much. Listening almost always expresses care much better than talking, whether on the phone or in person. When you call a person who is suffering, call with the intention of listening much more than talking.

## ASKING QUESTIONS

In person or on the telephone, questions can be either useful and caring or intrusive and burdensome. Here are a few principles for asking questions.

## *Ask Questions—and Then Listen*

Ask a question and then be patient. Give the person a chance to reflect and then respond. After asking a question, a tendency is often to rush to fill the silence that may occur while the other person ponders what you have asked. You might be tempted to ask another question or even answer the first one yourself. Anxiety can cause some people to ask one question after another without pausing for a response. So ask your questions, but then give the person time to think before responding.

Suffering people often want to talk about their situation and feelings and frequently will talk—if we let them. Good questions can open gushers, and then healing begins, in part because you are gaining information with which to help the person, but mostly because he or she is talking and you are listening.

## *Curb Your Curiosity*

Before asking a question of someone who is suffering, ask *yourself* a question: "Will knowing the answer to this question help me be a better caregiver?" One person mentioned how inappropriate questions disturbed her: "Probing questions were unwelcome when the questioner seemed more interested in the information than in me."

Questions seeking information unrelated to a hurting person's pain are better left unasked.

- A friend's daughter and boyfriend are seriously injured in an automobile crash. Don't ask, "Were they living together?"

- A coworker's husband has just died. Don't ask, "Are you going to sell your big house?"

Also avoid questions that sound as if you are placing blame or that might prompt "what if" scenarios in the hurting person's mind.

- A neighbor's teenage daughter dies in an automobile accident. Don't ask, "Was she wearing a seatbelt?"
- A friend's brother is diagnosed with lung cancer. Don't ask, "Is he a smoker?"

### Ask Open-Ended Questions

Knowing *how* to ask questions is as important as knowing what to ask. Open-ended questions provide an opportunity for more than a yes or no answer. Closed questions, on the other hand, can be quite sufficiently answered with a yes or no. They don't require much reflection or sharing. Here are examples of both types of questions.

Closed: Are you angry?
Open: How did you feel?

Closed: Do you need help?
Open: How can I help?

Closed: Are you overwhelmed?
Open: How are you feeling with all of this happening at once?

Closed: Are you going to _____?
Open: What are you thinking about doing?

Open-ended questions invite the hurting person to reflect, feel, and share more deeply.

## USING HUMOR

Exercise great sensitivity when you consider using humor with someone who is suffering. Humor can be a lift to the spirits or the ultimate in songs sung to a heavy heart. Consider the following four principles when you feel humor bubbling up.

### *Wait!*

The first—and most important—principle about using humor is as simple as this: Wait! Humor often can help in the healing process, but usually not at first. The initial shock has to wear off and sometimes physical healing needs to occur before hurting people can enjoy humor. One woman who was dealing with cancer said, "I didn't enjoy any humor relating to my illness. Humor has its own time and place, and when I was feeling poorly was not the time!" Another noted that ill-timed attempts at humor made her upset and angry.

Later—perhaps much later—the time may come when you can lighten your words and lift the other person's spirits with humor. Then, the next three principles apply.

### *Allow Humor to Develop Naturally*

When you're with a hurting person, you're there to care, not to be funny. Don't plan humor to use in your interaction. If humor is appropriate, it will come up naturally.

One individual described a situation that illustrates this principle: "I volunteered to take an uptight, elderly neighbor whom I didn't know well to the hospital for a colonoscopy to help her fill out forms. I couldn't help with the questions concerning what surgeries she'd had, the dates for them, and so on. I was certain, however, of the answer to one question: this 86-year-old widow was not pregnant. I couldn't help smiling as I said, 'Next question: Are you pregnant?' She knew I was kidding and laughed out loud."

Sometimes people are uncomfortable in a serious situation and try to force a joke to relieve the tension. Such forced humor may relieve the caregiver's anxiety, but it may deliver a serious blow to the one who is suffering. Right after her father died, one woman was subjected to forced humor. While the family was gathered around her mother, one sister-in-law kept making funny remarks, trying to lighten the moment. The mother said, "I don't know what she's laughing at. This is not a funny situation."

If you are present when someone forces humor into a serious situation, avoid jumping on the bandwagon. Perhaps you can check in later with the suffering person to make sure the forced humor has not squelched his or her need to talk about the painful situation. Your openness to accept the situation as it is might provide the boost to his or her spirits that the joking and humor couldn't supply.

### *Use Humor More Freely with Those You Know Well*

The closer your relationship with the hurting individual, the more likely your humor will be appropriate and appreciated. The story of one pastor spoke to this:

> When we were grieving the loss of our son, two of my wife's closest friends came to visit us. They wept with us and shared our pain. After a while, though, my wife lightened the mood with one of

those witty comments that only a close friend can fully appreciate. The two friends followed suit, and we all enjoyed a few minutes of lighthearted banter. To be honest, if it were anyone else I may have been upset by the jokes and the laughter. But somehow, with these two friends we both knew so well, it seemed right.

Another individual shared this insight: "A person must have earned the right to use humor with me." How do you earn that right? By sharing the hurt before even thinking about sharing the humor. One man offered his experience: "The person who came to console me used humor sparingly and gently. He also knew me and my situation well. I would have been offended if someone I knew only casually had responded to my pain with humor."

### *Follow the Sufferer's Lead*

Take your cues from the person experiencing pain and suffering. If he or she jokes or otherwise brings humor into the situation, it's probably all right for you to respond in kind. Just be careful that the joking isn't a desperate attempt by the hurting individual to hold back tears or other feelings that need to be released. Your responding with more jokes could cap those tears and feelings.

For the same reason, be careful not to take an inch of humor from the hurting person and immediately carry it a mile. Humor that lifts the spirits of the suffering person is usually best dispensed in small doses.

## SHARING READING MATERIALS

People often consider sharing reading materials to comfort or help those who are suffering. Here are some ways to maximize the benefits and minimize the hazards in your sharing.

### *Wait for the Initial Crisis or Shock to Pass*

In general, allow some time to pass before offering reading material. When someone has just been hit hard—a cancer diagnosis, for example—that person probably will not be interested in reading about cancer or anything else for a while. As one caregiver wisely noted, "People in pain don't want to read—they prefer to talk."

After everything settles down a bit, ask if the person wants to read a particular book or article. Phrase your question in such a way that the person feels free to say yes or no. "I read about this *[situation]* in an article a few days ago. I found it very informative. Would you like to see that article?" or "I read a book titled _____ that helped me in a similar situation. Would you like me to get you a copy?" Listen to the tone of the person's reply as well as the content. Does the person respond unenthusiastically? If so, wait and bring it up again later.

### *Share Material You Are Familiar With*

The most valuable kind of book or article to share is one you have read and benefited from. Impulse purchases based on a title that catches your eye tend to be least valuable.

Reading materials that are preachy or full of platitudes can also make hurting people think that you are criticizing them or implying that they aren't handling things right. "Personally, I read some books until they become dog-eared," one person shared, but she also added a warning: "They help only if they fit the despair I'm feeling and are not full of platitudes."

## Share Bite-Sized Morsels

Resources that make a few simple, focused, and well-organized points will probably be the most helpful to someone who is suffering. "Although reading was vital in my grieving," one woman wrote, "I could only read for short periods."

Reading material in which the reader has to wade through a great number of pages to find a gem or understand the point is less helpful. Research participants agreed: the shorter the better. Marking some areas in reading material can be helpful to someone who is having difficulty concentrating, but avoid appearing preachy or judgmental in what you mark. One man noted, "When my friend marked spots in the book that he had found encouraging, I could focus on those areas first. But I didn't like it if somebody marked up a book so I would 'get the point.'"

## Give Rather Than Lend

Give reading materials to the suffering person; don't lend them. This relieves the stress of trying to remember who lent what and saves the person the trouble of having to return the material. One person noted, "When people gave books to me, I could turn to them and read them when I was ready.

I still have some of those books and read them whenever I'm having a hard time."

Sharing reading materials is not a simple task. Think carefully about such sharing because what you share will reflect *you* to the suffering person.

## ASSURING PEOPLE OF GOD'S LOVE

Providing guidelines for this last caring action—assuring people of God's love—may strike you as odd. Since Christians are called to share God's love with others, how could such assurances ever be out of place? Certainly, God's love is powerful and valuable. This section simply encourages you to *care-fully* think through *when, how,* and *why* you are sharing such assurances.

Research confirmed that assurances of God's love can either be very powerful or they can come across as empty or even counterproductive. Here are some principles that can help determine whether such assurances would be beneficial to a hurting person.

### *Be Sure You're Fulfilling the Sufferer's Need to Hear Assurance, Not Your Need to Share It*

Sometimes when caregivers assure others of God's love, they are actually trying to reassure *themselves*. They may be struggling with their own faith and feelings about God. Maybe they are questioning God's love because they feel uncomfortable seeing someone else suffer. If it's really *your* need to hear the assurance rather than the hurting person's, it's best not to bounce those words off a suffering person just so you can hear them.

### *Don't Offer Assurance When Someone Is Angry with God*

If you interject assurances of God's love when the other person is angry at God, you can actually harm his or her relationship with God. Those angry feelings need to come out. If you try to drown them out with assurances of God's love, you're interrupting a good and healthy venting process that needs to take place. You're singing songs to an *angry* heart.

Wait until later to offer assurance. In time the individual may come to a deep and comforting reassurance of God's love even before you offer any verbal assurance. But first the person's anger must work itself out.

### *If a Hurting Person Asks about God's Love, Don't Answer . . . Yet*

If the person you are relating to asks whether God loves him or her, don't jump in with a quick assurance. Wait. Listen. Now, I'm not suggesting you play games with a suffering person. But if the individual is asking about God's love, he or she probably is struggling, and a hasty assurance of God's love may have the opposite effect from what you intend. One man shared his experience with hasty assurances: "I found many people who were ready to say their 'lines' to me, but few that asked about or listened to what my needs were." Another person said that assurances "often felt like 'pat answers.' Often people seemed unable to cope with my intense sadness."

When a suffering individual seems to ask for the assurance of God's love, the best reply may actually be another question: "I'd like to know what you are thinking right now.

Can you tell me about that?" Give the person an opportunity to talk about these thoughts and feelings. Then share an assurance, if it's still needed.

The best result occurs, however, when the suffering person can talk, maybe weep, perhaps even rant, but then comes to his or her own positive conclusion about God's love and shares that conclusion with you. Then you'll know God's love is rooted deep in that person's heart.

## Be God's Love

Words of assurance are not the only way to let people know that God loves them. You can *be* God's love to another. One person shared, "I have mostly *felt* God's love through someone's care and presence and acceptance, not from their words."

Both you and the hurting individual are objects of God's love. You know it to be true in your own life, and you can convey it to others by your caring actions.

# 9

# WORDS THAT HURT,
# NOT HEAL

*Lord, curb my clichés. When a platitude wants to pop
out, put a plug in it for me. Stifle my simple fixes of
others' hurts. Let my words be yours, and speak the
loving care of Christ through me, which is what you want
those who are suffering to hear. Amen.*

Some words nearly always wound people who are suffering. This chapter describes the words and phrases that research showed hurt the most. These platitudes, clichés, and other expressions are words that hurt rather than heal, even when people say them with the kindest intentions.

Chances are good that you'll find statements here that others have offered to you as comfort. As one participant put it, "I have certainly heard enough clichés to last a lifetime." You probably have too. Maybe these statements have hurt you. They may have made you angry. You're in good company, because research participants were nearly universal in their negative reactions to these statements.

You may recognize words here that you have offered in an attempt to be caring. That happens to the best of us. Everyone—no exceptions—makes mistakes.

You might think, "But I say some of these statements all the time, and I never get a bad reaction." Consider the possibility that you have experienced another person's *polite silence*. When faced with empty platitudes, one research participant said, "I shut down, zone out, fuzz focus, and wear a polite but cold smile." Hurting people who receive such statements commonly respond this way—they nod passively and keep quiet. Inside, however, they may be seething. Polite silence is far from acceptance.

Here are seven statements to avoid at all costs.

## "I Know How You Feel"

Not one research participant liked the statement "I know how you feel." They liked "I know *just* how you feel" even less, and "I know *exactly* how you feel" even less than that.

This universal rejection sends a clear message: Don't say these words! People's dislike of this type of statement makes perfect sense when you stop to think about it. No one knows how you feel, and you don't know how anyone else feels. You may think you know, you may guess how someone else feels, you may suppose you know how someone else feels, but it's all speculation. And in speculating, you rob the other of his or her unique identity.

People object to being robbed. It upsets them, and when they are already suffering, the last thing you want to do is add to their pain. One person shared this reaction: "The statement that someone else knows how I feel is the hardest one to listen to. No one knows how I feel. My reaction was very negative to such a statement, and now I just say, 'No, you don't,' which may seem abrupt, but it sure helps me."

This is an honest and healthy response. If every suffering person had the strength to respond this way, then "I know how you feel" would be snuffed out in no time.

Denying yourself the right to say "I know how you feel" does not mean you have to abandon empathy. *Empathy* is "feeling with" the other person, which suggests that first you should find out how he or she feels. There is all the difference in the world between saying, "I know how you feel" and asking, "How are you feeling?"

Depending on the circumstances and the individual you are talking with, later in your relating you may be able to say, "I was in a situation somewhat similar to the one you are in now, and I remember at that time feeling _____." This is far different from saying, "I know how you feel." You are instead saying, "I remember how I felt," which you can safely assert.

## "IT'S FOR THE BEST"

If your goal is to care for and comfort a suffering person, don't say, "It's for the best." Without exception, research participants who had experienced pain and suffering reported that words like these were hurtful, not healing.

Here are a number of other oft-heard statements that communicate much the same thing and should be avoided:

- "He's at peace now."
- "Well, you know she's in a better place."

- "It's good he's not suffering anymore."
- "She's with Jesus now."
- "He's better off."
- "It's a blessing."

It's easy to understand why people latch onto this sentiment when seeking to comfort others. It's cheery. It looks on the bright side. It may even be insightful. But the problem is that, instead of viewing the situation from the suffering person's perspective, these statements admonish him or her to see the situation from the caregiver's point of view. Even when such a view might be true, "It's for the best" statements are better left unsaid until the hurting person arrives at that conclusion independently.

## "Keep a Stiff Upper Lip"

To a woman after a miscarriage: "You already have three children. You don't have enough bedrooms anyway."

To someone just divorced: "Go on, have a good time and get over it."

To a woman having emergency surgery and facing hospitalization for ten days, a relative said: "You never could tolerate pain—it's not that bad."

To a man who lost his job: "What doesn't kill you makes you stronger."

Statements like these are meant to encourage hurting people to "keep a stiff upper lip and take it like a man." But this kind of tough talk chafes the sensibilities of the one who is suffering. No one likes it. That's a sweeping statement, but the research bears it out. Of those who were offered such statements as comfort, 98% said they did not like them.

Often statements like these pile unrealistic and unhealthy expectations on the one hurting. Someone told a man whose wife was dying, "I have a friend who is in a situation similar to yours, and he is at peace with that situation." Listen to the message within that message: "Why can't you respond to your situation the way my friend responds to his situation?" A person who makes statements like these might as well have said, "You are handling your suffering all wrong. Let me tell you how to do it" or "You are weak."

The "keep a stiff upper lip" expressions imply that the hurting person needs to get through this situation and move on quickly. Unspoken is the subtle directive, "Now it's time for your pain and suffering to be over." Consider this: How long should suffering last? How long should it be tolerated? And the answer is, *much longer than people think or are willing to tolerate.* Harmful words like "You've got to get on with your life" are too often said to those who are suffering.

The most helpful words are those that allow a hurting person time to heal. As a woman whose brother had died of a heroin overdose said, "One person told me to take my time in the grieving process. This meant so much to me because others tried to rush me." A recently divorced person felt this same sense of relief: "It was helpful to be told, 'Give yourself time to grieve.'"

## "AT LEAST . . . "

About a month after Joan died, an acquaintance I hadn't talked with in years called to say he was sorry to hear about her death. After talking for a few minutes, he mentioned that his wife too had died of ovarian cancer. In the course of the conversation, he asked me how long I had been married. I said, "Thirty-three years." He told me that he had been married 64 years. I could have said—and I admit I was thinking it—"At least you got over 50 years," or "You had 31 years more than I did," or "Sixty-four years is pretty good." I'm pretty sure that a comment from me on his more-than-average number of years of marriage would not have set well with him. If he had said that he had enjoyed 64 good years and was thankful for it, then it would have been appropriate for me to agree. But it would not have been helpful for me to bring it up, and, thankfully, I had enough wits to refrain from doing so.

The problem with "at least" statements is that they tend to minimize the pain of the suffering person by saying that it's not as bad as it could be or that other people have experienced worse. Most hurting people react negatively to having the significance of their pain diminished, and that's why at-least statements are so hurtful.

If hurting people make at-least statements, you can certainly affirm them. But wait for them to say it first. A woman whose father died of cancer said, "I'm glad he's out of his misery now, but boy, do I miss him!" You *could* affirm her statement about his being out of his misery since she brought it up, but you certainly *should* respond to her missing her father.

At-least statements may come to mind at times as you relate to hurting people. You're not likely to eradicate at-least statements completely from your thinking. Perhaps a good principle is: It's all right to *think* at-least thoughts; it's not all right to *say* them.

## "YOU SHOULD/SHOULDN'T . . ."

People *should* on others all the time. You've probably had it done to you, and maybe you've done it to others.

*Shoulds* and *shouldn'ts* reveal what one person thinks another should or shouldn't do; or they communicate how another should or shouldn't feel. Either way, when *shoulds* are laid on a suffering person, it not only is an unpleasant experience, but also tends to shut down communication.

Here are some examples shared by research participants of the ways *should* was expressed to them:

- A person who had relocated, leaving her hometown of 31 years: "They said that I needed to look at it as a new adventure; that I'd enjoy the challenge; that it was past time for me to make a move; that I'd love it if I gave it a chance."
- A few weeks after the death of a son: "You need to get over it and get on with your life."
- A sibling told one woman who was going through a divorce: "You ought to have left years ago! You can't let this ruin your life."

You can *should* on someone without actually saying the word. *You ought to, you need to, you can't* . . . these phrases all communicate much the same message.

Sometimes the *should* may even be right. It might be better for a hurting person to change certain attitudes or to take specific actions. The point is not whether the person should have certain attitudes or take certain actions. The point is that these kinds of words only bring more suffering to the hurting person, so it's better not to say them.

One man who had gone through a divorce said, "There were those who always gave me quick-fix solutions, telling me what I should do. Instead I withdrew and retreated even more." A woman said, "It was harmful, people telling me what I should do. My response was to stop discussing things with those people. I resented them for making me feel as if I had to do what they wanted."

*The five statements covered so far in this chapter could be called "secular" platitudes, words commonly used throughout society. Platitudes cloaked in religious language become even more damaging because they appear to carry the weight of religious authority. Two of the most pervasive —and painful—religious platitudes follow.*

## "GOD DOESN'T GIVE YOU ANY MORE THAN YOU CAN HANDLE"

Where in the Bible does it say that money is the root of all evil? Nowhere. In 1 Timothy 6:10 Paul says that the *love* of money is the root of all evil, not money itself.

Where in the Bible is the book of Hezekiah? Nowhere. Hezekiah, one of the kings of Judah, is mentioned in the Old Testament books of 2 Kings, 2 Chronicles, and Isaiah, but there is no book named after him in the Bible.

Where in the Bible does it say about the early Christians, "See how they love one another"? Nowhere. These words are not in the Bible; they were written by Tertullian, an early church theologian and apologist.[1]

Where in the Bible does it say, "God doesn't give you more than you can handle"? Nowhere. It simply doesn't.

Although this statement is often quoted as biblical truth, the Bible does not state this. It is loosely based on 1 Corinthians 10:13:

> No temptation has seized you except what is common to man. And God is faithful; he will not let you be tempted beyond what you can bear. But when you are tempted, he will also provide a way out so that you can stand up under it.

Many suffering people who hear "God doesn't give you any more than you can handle" will immediately accept it as having the ring of truth and the unquestionable authority of Holy Scripture because the statement is so similar in tone to 1 Corinthians 10:13. It is both a mistranslation and a mis-interpretation of that passage.

A careful reading of the passage reveals that this verse is not at all about bearing up under pain and suffering but about resisting temptation. In fact, in 1 Corinthians 10:13 Paul does not use any of the Greek words for pain, suffering, or sorrow that he uses elsewhere in his writings. The specific word he chooses is the one that is used for "temptation" throughout the New Testament—*peirosmòs,* the same word found in the Lord's Prayer where Jesus says, "And lead us not into *temptation"* (Matthew 6:13; Luke 11:4).

In addition to the meaning of the Greek word, the context of the verse clearly indicates that Paul is talking about temptation, not suffering. The children of Israel, he says, had been tempted to follow false gods in the months after the Exodus. He encourages the Corinthians to avoid making the same mistake that the Israelites did and promises that

God will help them bear up under the temptation to return to false gods.

"God doesn't give you any more than you can handle" has another problem as well—the "God gives you" part. First Corinthians 10:13 doesn't say that God tempts people, and it certainly doesn't say that God gives people pain and suffering. Why add to the burden of a hurting person by saying that God is causing the suffering?

Of the research participants who had been told by others, "God doesn't give you any more than you can handle," 88% reacted negatively. One suffering person said, "In the depth of my pain, I really believed God had made a serious mistake. I was so depressed that I could barely get out of bed." The simple fact is that those who are suffering often feel their burden is too great to bear. How painful it must be to hear someone diminish their pain or imply that they're in good hands because God is the one causing their suffering. "To me, this is a remarkably unfeeling and unsympathetic statement—as though the person is saying that I had no right to feel sad or despairing," one person stated.

Several noted that they were tired of the platitude and had learned to respond forthrightly to those who say it. "Then God has overestimated me" is one response. Another says, "I may have reached my limit!" Another asserts, "I think God has me mixed up with somebody else."

One woman who had watched a parent die after a protracted battle with cancer pointed out an additional fallacy in this kind of statement: "'God never gives you a burden you can't carry' . . . so if I were weaker, this wouldn't have happened!"

## "IT'S GOD'S WILL"

One of the most carelessly used religious phrases purporting to offer comfort is "It's God's will." Of the research participants who had been told that their suffering was God's will, 93% reacted strongly and negatively. Some were quite outspoken in their reaction. A typical response was, "It took me years to work through my anger toward God and much prayer and personal study to figure out that God is there to *help* us through our issues, and that God cries when we cry."

The purpose here is not to debate the various theological points and positions about what the true will of God is, but to assert that the theological wrangling or the pronouncements that arise from such wrangling have little place in caregiving. Such arguing isn't likely to comfort a hurting person. "When people talked to me about my pain being 'God's will' or a 'divine plan,' I felt devastated," one woman stated. "It seemed like my pain was not valued in God's overall scheme of things, that it was just minor or trivial to Him."

One implication of such comments is that the hurting person should not feel the way he or she is feeling. "It's God's will" is often a way of minimizing or explaining away feelings and hurts. Many things *do* hurt, and that's reality. To try to lessen hurts by explaining them as part of God's plan is to deny the right that we have as humans *and as Christians* to feel what we feel. As one man indicated, "These are not helpful words. To me, they convey 'I don't know what the heck to say, so just don't cry on me,' or 'Hurry up and accept it, so I don't have to hear or see your pain.'"

The small percentage of people in the research who seemed to find "It's God's will" acceptable usually had gone through less serious life crises—shorter term, fully recoverable, involving no lifestyle changes. They often were reflecting back on an event that had turned out all right. Rarely, if ever, was a "will of God" explanation received well when significant and irreparable loss had occurred.

Whatever your particular beliefs about God's will, remember that it's always easier to view a painful situation as somehow part of God's will when you are not the one suffering. You might believe that you can assist a hurting person by helping him or her to see the situation "from God's perspective." But who of us can see any situation wholly from God's perspective? As Doug Manning writes, "God does not gossip. He does not talk about you to others. No matter how convincing they sound, they do not know the will of God for you."[2]

In contrast to the hurtful words like those in this chapter, consider this example from a woman whose 22-year-old son died in an accidental fall: "Young people who had known our son were so stricken that they needed to gather together and asked to be with us. While this was difficult, it was an amazing presence for us. They were surprisingly able to avoid platitudes and knew the value of just being together in our sorrow."

When bad things happen, people don't need platitudes and clichés. They need to be able to lean on each other and support one another.

# 10

# PINK THINKING

*Dear Lord, I want my presence to be a help, not a hindrance. Help me make it so. Help me relate to suffering people honestly, being good and true to their needs. Without your watching over my tendencies to evade and avoid, I can't do it, Lord. Thank you for guarding me from my own discomfort. In the name of your caring Son Jesus. Amen.*

The difference between "words that hurt, not heal" in the last chapter and "pink thinking" in this chapter is the difference between being harpooned and being nibbled to death by ducks. The hurting words in the last chapter are "in-your-face" and openly wounding; the words and behaviors in this chapter are more subtle but can be just as harmful to a hurting person.

Pink thinking is optimism run amok. Pink thinking denies the reality of an individual's suffering and glosses over the hurting person's pain. The pink thinker seeks to

banish any dark and gloomy thoughts and urges the suffering one to "think positive" regardless of the situation.

Pink thinkers believe their role is to prod suffering
individuals out of their quagmire of despair and propel them
to heights of hopefulness. "Look on the bright side!" is their
banner as they try to buoy up hurting people instead of
meeting them at their place of pain.

Here are some ways you can keep pink thinking from
sneaking in and sabotaging your caring efforts.

## CHEERING PEOPLE UP

On the face of it, "cheering people up" sounds like a good
thing to do. More often than not, however, trying to cheer up
people who are hurting makes them feel even worse.
Research participants stressed this consistently and repeat-
edly as they thought back to times when they personally had
experienced pain and suffering.

One person said, "When someone tries to cheer me up
when I'm suffering, it makes me feel worse. I need someone
just 'to be' rather than to talk or tell me what I should be
doing and feeling." Another said, "I felt they did not hear me,
and therefore, they didn't understand. Were they really interested in my situation or did they just want me to hurry up
and *get over it?"*

One way people attempt to cheer others up is by urging
them to "look on the bright side." Where did the idea come
from that Christians must smile all the time? Why should
Christians expect that life will be uninterrupted bliss? As one
woman said:

When I was in the depths of grief, there wasn't any bright side. I didn't want to hear about hope or about anything that might make me 'feel better' because I needed to experience the feelings at the point where I was. Encouragement for me came in that I was not alone in suffering, that people all throughout Scripture felt the same kinds of feelings that I did, and that friends now were willing to sit with me in the midst of my suffering.

One hazard of setting out to cheer up suffering people is that you may create a yo-yo effect in their emotions. Even if the cheering up seems to work for the moment, a letdown usually follows as soon as you walk out the door. Cheering up is an artificial high. As one research participant noted, "It *[cheering up]* just slapped a bandage on my struggle."

One caregiver recognized what often happens: "If you try to cheer up people, the plusses are mostly for yourself." Cheering up is often a way that caregivers try to make themselves feel better. The suffering person is left feeling weighed down by an additional, unnecessary burden—the burden of trying to make the supposed caregiver feel better. One woman who was grieving the loss of a sibling expressed it this way: "I felt I had to respond artificially, even for that moment, so I wouldn't disappoint them or make them feel they had failed." Another person agreed: "When people tried to cheer me up, it would upset me. It told me that it was not okay to be hurting because it made them uncomfortable." Still another added very truthfully, "I wanted to smack them!"

Cheering up the suffering is a subtle yet powerful expectation that misleads many caregivers into thinking, *If I leave and this hurting person is not more cheerful than when I walked in, I have failed.* But cheering up may instead signal suffering people that it's not acceptable for them to feel what they are feeling or to respond as they have responded. It's like hanging out a sign that says, "Authentic feelings not welcome here."

## GLOSSING OVER

*Glossing over* is a form of pink thinking behavior that minimizes or trivializes suffering. "It's not so bad," someone may say to a hurting person. Such insensitive behavior robs the suffering person of something he or she deeply needs: the acknowledgment that his or her suffering is real and significant. "When people acted like what happened to me was no big deal," one individual remembers, "I wanted to scream, 'That's easy for you to say! Would you like to try this experience for yourself?'"

Another person said that glossing over "takes away your self-worth because it makes you feel that your situation is no big deal and you just need to 'snap out of it!'"

Glossing over often takes the form of an easy assurance that everything is going to be all right. Research participants reported that they found the following phrases particularly unhelpful or even hurtful:

- "You'll get over this in no time!"
- "I had the same thing—it was not that bad."
- "Just trust in God. It will get better."

- "You're young. You'll marry again."
- "You'll make new friends."
- "You'll be fine."
- "There are other people worse off than you."

Words like these can sound patronizing to a hurting individual and make it clear that the caregiver is not acknowledging the pain.

## DENIAL

When a suffering person first experiences a shock, denial can be a natural and healthy way of dealing with the immediate pain. Sometimes, however, the hurting person perceives the situation realistically, but others around him or her refuse to acknowledge the truth or to allow the hurting person to do so.

One individual told this story about her visit with a friend who was dying from cancer. The friend was under hospice care at home, having stopped all but palliative treatment. "We were just sitting there around her bed, family members and a few friends. My dying friend looked at all of us and said a little wistfully, 'I'm sure going to miss you guys!' Immediately, one of the group shot back, 'We're still hoping for a miracle.' I felt so bad because my friend's attempt to tell us good-bye was interrupted by someone who just couldn't face reality." Certainly one can always hope for a miracle, but denying the reality of that painful situation also denied the suffering person the privilege of talking about what was happening and how she felt about it.

Denial springs from the same root as other forms of pink thinking: the caregiver's discomfort when faced with another's pain and suffering. Denial is not just proposing an alternative view of a situation. Rather, it's the unwillingness to acknowledge and accept the reality that the suffering person is recognizing and sharing.

When asked how they responded to the denial of their suffering on the part of others, most people answered the same way: "I felt very hurt," "I avoided that person," "I turned away," "I withdrew," "I didn't talk with that person about it anymore."

One man, though, told of the most helpful statement anyone had made after the death of his mother: "Heaven rejoices; earth sorrows." That simple statement acknowledged the whole truth of the situation while denying nothing. It affirmed the peace that the mother now knew, but acknowledged the grief of those left behind.

## TOUGH ENCOURAGEMENT

You've probably seen cheerleaders at a football game encouraging the players on the field to greater effort, to win at all costs. Tough encouragement is a form of pink thinking that dismisses another's pain with forced and false cheerleading, declaring that the suffering one just needs to be strong or to "Fight, Fight, Fight!"

A college student whose mother had a neuromuscular disease told of some so-called comfort she received, which was really no comfort at all. She had come home for the summer to discover that her mother's condition had worsened since spring vacation. She was understandably sad and afraid.

The student sought out a youth leader at church whom she knew from her high school days. Early in the conversation, the youth leader said, "I know that whatever happens, you'll do well. I know that you're a strong individual. I have confidence in you."

"This was not what I needed to hear," the student said later in recounting this story. "I didn't feel strong. I didn't want to hear that I would do well. I just wanted someone to listen to me and let me get it all out."

Someone once told a research participant: "I can't think of a person better able to handle this suffering than you." Such tough encouragement is rarely encouraging and is usually quite frightening to a hurting person. "When a person is vulnerable," asserted one focus group member, *"'strong'* is not a comforting word." Another person agreed: "Most of the time it's tactless, flippant, theological babble because the speaker is uncomfortable with the other person's pain."

The research shows that hurting people clearly do not appreciate being told that they are strong. They need the time and the opportunity to be weak, perhaps letting someone else be strong at that point in time. Sometimes they need permission to be weak, not forced to be strong.

I met a woman in church at coffee hour who hadn't attended worship for two years. In the course of our conversation, I learned that her sister had recently died of cancer, her mother was in a nursing home suffering from Alzheimer's disease, and she was going through a divorce. She concluded this catalog of horrors with a brave front: "But I'm strong. I can take it. I'll manage somehow."

"I admire your strength," I told her, "but it's okay to be weak, too. That's one of the reasons we have each other in the church—to help bear one another's burdens." I'm pretty sure that she had come back to church because she needed to be around people who would allow her to be weak, to be in a place where people believed in bearing one another's burdens.

## UNBRIDLED CELEBRATING

"Celebrating victories, whether big or small, helps to create hope," asserted one research participant. Another person illustrated some of the reasons to celebrate: "A celebration can be such a small thing: a smile after crying, a few steps out to the garden, going out to eat, playing with the dog again, having the strength to get to church. All the little daily things warrant celebration." And remember Paul's exhortation in Romans 12:15: "Rejoice with those who rejoice; mourn with those who mourn." So don't forget to rejoice with people.

If celebrating is such a good thing, then why discuss it as a potential area of pink thinking? Because *celebrating* victories *with* a hurting person is quite different from *forcing* celebrations *onto* a suffering individual.

"It was hard to celebrate victories when my suffering expanded to crowd out everything else. Victories seemed trivial at those times," one research participant said. Another agreed: "I was unable to celebrate small or large victories while in the depths of pain and despair. It made me feel worse because I felt unaffirmed in my pain and even felt guilty for not wishing to celebrate."

Against the backdrop of great suffering, these individuals did not feel like celebrating even a small victory. That's fine. The key is to discover whether a hurting person actually wants to celebrate a particular "victory." You can offer celebratory words—once. Perhaps gently say, "That's very nice," with a smile but without a lot of fanfare. You're testing the waters to see if the hurting person wants to celebrate. If you start with a little celebration and the individual doesn't respond, stop celebrating immediately. To continue would be to sing a full oratorio to a heavy heart.

Sometimes caregivers try to create or celebrate victories that may not be real or important to the hurting person. As one woman noted, "When I was suffering, I didn't want anyone to try to make me celebrate victories. I had to work through the hurt before I could see the good."

That's why it's so important to allow the hurting person to initiate any celebration. "There were problems when I did not initiate the celebration of a victory, whatever it was," a pastor said. "I only wanted to share the victory with those I trusted, who would not have unrealistic expectations of more such victories."

Hurting people often see themselves as broken and others as whole. Pink thinking behaviors that gloss over, deny, or in any way minimize the painful reality of a suffering person only reinforce this perception. Banishing pink thinking opens the door to caring for hurting people in more meaningful and genuinely comforting ways.

# 11

# CREATING A SAFE PLACE

*Dear Lord, I don't want to close up if someone tells me
bad news. Help me radiate acceptance and love to hurting people, no matter what they find the courage to tell
me. Thank you for giving me unchanging love no matter
what I tell you. In Jesus' name. Amen.*

"So, how are you?"

"Fine."

I have a friend in Alcoholics Anonymous who tells me
that in that organization, *fine* as a response to "How are
you?" is taken to mean, "*F*ouled up, *I*nsecure, *N*eurotic, and
*E*mpty." Because of this, he now responds to people who tell
him they are "fine" with, "Oh, that bad, eh?"

Why do we waste our time with such empty exchanges?
"How are you?" "Fine." *I don't tell you how I'm doing
because I don't think you are interested. Or I don't think you
have time. Or I don't believe you'll accept me if I tell you
how things are really going with me, which, incidentally, is
not all that great.*

*Truthfully, it's worse than that. It's bad. Things are not going well at all for me. But if I tell you the truth, what will you do? Will you turn away from me? Will you leave me alone with my furies, my despair, my loneliness? I can imagine all kinds of scenarios, and most of them are pretty bleak.*

You have it within your power to create a safe place for those who are suffering. What a precious gift you give to hurting people when they know they can talk with you and truly be accepted.

## THE ECONOMY OF PAIN AND SUFFERING

How much energy do hurting persons spend covering up their feelings? How high is the cost of "putting on a happy face"?

Hiding feelings takes much more energy than being straightforward—and suffering people don't have a lot of energy to spare. They need their energy to cope with the circumstances of their pain. They can waste a lot of energy worrying about how others will react to their pain. Hurting people should not have to carry that burden.

One research participant said, "I just wound up telling them what they wanted to hear. I think they left feeling better, but I felt worse." Another said, "I felt I needed to hide my suffering, so I would appear to be a person of faith." That's quite a load for a hurting person to carry.

I learned a valuable lesson about the economy of pain and suffering at a particularly difficult time in Joan's battle with cancer. One treatment option after another was being closed to her, and she was experiencing a succession of serious physical problems connected with the progressing cancer. In the midst of these dark days, a friend from out of town phoned. When I told him about these problems, he asked me, "Have you had anything good happen in the past week?" I replied, "In all honesty, no." He drew a deep breath and answered, "That's really rough. I'm so sorry to hear that." Our conversation quickly moved to a deeper and more meaningful level.

Not only did his words give me permission to be honest with him in that conversation, but I found that in the following days, weeks, and months, his words had empowered me to be much more honest when others asked me how things were going or how I was feeling. I quickly discovered, of course, that some people could not handle the unedited truth, but when others could deal with my increased openness, I found that we all benefited.

That's why your ability to take bad news as well as good is such a gift to a suffering individual. Your openness to that person's truth—whatever it might be—gives him or her permission to be honest, to share freely, to save valuable energy. Sharing openly and honestly about being "not so fine" can actually be energizing.

## PROGRESS

Movement, progress, change—these are important values in many areas of present-day society. For example, we expect highway construction crews to quickly finish the repairs that are tying up two of the three eastbound lanes on a major highway.

But imposing an expectation of progress on someone in the midst of a life crisis is counterproductive. "Come on, hurry up, get better." That sort of a message tells the suffering person it's not safe to reveal any bad news, only good. "How are you?" "Fine."

One woman who suffered from depression found that "if people didn't think I was doing better, they just wouldn't ask me anymore. They would pretend that nothing was wrong. I felt that they really didn't care about me at all." Another noted that it didn't matter what she said to those who asked how she was doing: "Usually they would smile, nod their head in the affirmative, and say something like 'Are you doing any better?' or 'It's great to see you feeling better' or 'I can see you're trusting God in this' and carry on with their conversation, even though I hadn't said anything of the kind."

Suffering frequently is not pretty. It may not be pretty emotionally, and sometimes it is not pretty physically. That makes relating to hurting individuals even harder. As one woman said about people who came to visit her husband near the end of his struggle with cancer, "It really put mortality right there in front of them. And that made it very difficult for them."

Some research participants discovered that even though they were suffering, others still expected them to "look good." One said, "It seemed that if I looked good, then they could believe I was getting better and that made *them* feel better." Another added, "I felt that it was important to others that I looked well because then they thought I needed less from them." A woman who had lost her handicapped son spoke to the heart of this whole issue: "Most people just can't let someone who is suffering work through it. It seems to be difficult to accept that it is 'normal' for a person to reflect inward pain with a sad outward appearance."

Is it wrong, then, to tell hurting people that they look good? Absolutely not. The problem arises if they sense that they have to look good to be acceptable to you.

Expecting progress or—worse—pushing for progress when there is none leaves suffering people feeling lonely and isolated. Wanting them to look good or to have a good attitude about their situation leaves them feeling frustrated or hopeless. It is far better for you to join them on their journey, wherever you find them, whatever their condition, and create a safe environment where honesty and openness can flourish.

## HEART OVER HEAD

When someone shares hard news with you, it means he or she is hurting. Go ahead and react emotionally to the news. That's being real. Respond from your heart.

Sharing often happens on the spur of the moment, which gives you little opportunity to think things through before responding. You may feel uneasy, uncertain of how to proceed or what to say in such a painful situation. This is the time to go against every temptation to put a positive spin on the news ("I know you will be able to handle this") or share a word of wisdom ("You just need to take it one day at a time"). These are "head" responses to a situation that requires your heart.

The research surfaced a number of "heart" responses that care receivers particularly welcomed.

- "I'm so sorry."
- "That's terrible!"
- "Bummer!"
- "Oh, no!"
- "I was hoping it would be different."

What you say depends on your own style and manner of speaking, your relationship with the hurting person, and the situation. You would be more likely to say "Bummer!" to someone who has scraped the fender of a new car. "Oh, no!" might be your response to someone reporting that he or she has suffered a serious medical setback.

Your initial response to people's bad news can be very powerful. A "head" response can communicate that their status is unacceptable and that good news is what you are looking for and all you really will accept. A "heart" response can let them know that your heart is right there with their heart—it's safe for them to be who they are with you.

## BODY LANGUAGE

"People let me know they were with me by their body language as much as by their words," said one woman. Body language is important in face-to-face relating to a suffering individual. One person humorously but truthfully noted postures to avoid when someone is telling you about a painful situation. "Here's what not to do: look bored as if you are now obligated to listen to troubles you don't want to hear. Look alarmed as if you're going to drop on the spot. Shift uneasily in your chair as if you're going to bolt momentarily."

Instead, when someone is sharing a genuine glimpse into his or her struggles or pain, lean closer to that person. By moving physically closer, you show your intent to be completely present for the other. As much as possible maintain eye contact with the hurting person, a gentle, steady gaze that says you're right there with him or her. Communicate your understanding and your willingness to continue listening with a nod or an occasional affirming sound.

Prayer can help you create a safe place. As you listen, silently ask God to help you love the hurting person unconditionally.

## REALLY REAL

If you know the suffering individual well, you can feel more at ease about getting "real" with him or her. Perhaps you have asked a good friend, "How are you doing?" and he or she has replied with a ritualistic "Fine." You might follow up by saying, "How are you *really* doing?" Or you could include the word *really* the first time you ask.

This simple but powerful word—*really*—shows your true interest in what the good friend has to say. Don't mouth this phrase casually or flippantly. Only say this if you truly want to know the answer.

Social conditioning teaches hurting people to hide their pain by responding with a brief, noncommunicative answer or giving a lot of peripheral information that doesn't get to the heart of their suffering. They've probably received enough negative feedback to be wary of saying anything not considered socially acceptable. But when you use the almost magical phrase—"Tell me how you're *really* doing"—a hurting individual is more likely to give you an honest answer because you have shown that you really want to hear the truth, no matter what that truth may be.

## DEMONSTRATING ACCEPTANCE

Acceptance of another person is a matter of "deep, empathic understanding," as Carl Rogers terms it, which allows you to see the world the other person inhabits through his or her eyes. Rogers says, "It means a respect and liking for [the person] as a separate person. . . . It means an acceptance of and regard for his [or her] attitudes of the moment, no matter how negative or positive."[1]

Sometimes caregivers give off subtle signals of non-acceptance, and suffering people are quick to pick up on such signals. "I felt rejected," said one person, "because I knew people did not want to hear about the negative things in my life." Another said, "After the death of our teenage son in a car accident, people would avoid us at church. Some of these people had known us for years. You could see them avert their eyes so as not to make eye contact."

Following his wife's death, C. S. Lewis found that people avoided him instead of accepting him in his sorrow:

> An odd byproduct of my loss is that I'm aware
> of being an embarrassment to everyone I meet.
> At work, at the club, in the street, I see people,
> as they approach me, trying to make up their

minds whether they'll "say something about it" or not. . . . Perhaps the bereaved ought to be isolated in special settlements like lepers.[2]

How can you demonstrate acceptance of a person's bad news?

- *Meet the person where he or she is.* Wherever the suffering person is—the pain level, feeling level, struggling level, sadness level—that's where you need to be. Trying to move your interaction with a hurting person to any other level is merely singing songs to a heavy heart.

- *Focus on the here and now rather than the there and then.* One woman said that she felt accepted because the person who talked with her "met with me in that moment, not in the future." It's a waste of time and breath to tell a hurting individual, "You will feel better as time goes on." The person is hurting right now and probably can't see beyond this moment's pain. Keep your focus on the present and on the pain.

- *Acknowledge the feelings.* The dominant part of a hurting person's framework is the set of mostly negative feelings swirling around inside. Respond to that individual in a feeling way rather than an intellectual way. When one woman was overwhelmed with grief at her loss, she said, "One of the most helpful things anyone said to me was that I would undoubtedly have all manner of thoughts and feelings, some of which would seem terrible to me, but that I should just accept them and not bother with guilt."

The results of such acceptance are little short of miraculous. This is the sunshine of *agape* love, and it creates a warm, safe place where comfort can grow in the other person. This is what you want to happen in your caregiving.

## AVOIDING AVOIDANCE

So far, the focus has been on how hurting people benefit when you create a safe place, where bad news as well as good news is accepted. But *you* also benefit from being able to accept any kind of news a suffering individual may share.

One person in the research commented: "When a couple in my congregation were grieving the death of their young child, I didn't know what to say to them. So when I would see them at a distance, I avoided contact with them. I felt terrible about that, but I just didn't know what to do or say."

You give a great gift when you create relationships where hurting people feel safe enough to be honest, easily and naturally. You also receive a great gift: the other person's trust and gratitude, the privilege of journeying with the suffering person, the knowledge that you had the courage to care, and the miracle of being God incarnate to another human being. When you create a safe place for a suffering person, he or she may pay you a high compliment by gratefully saying, "I can be honest with you." What a privilege!

# 12

# SIMPLE AND PROFOUND

*Dear God, relating to those who suffer is profoundly holy work. Help me to keep the pure simplicity of it ever in mind, and keep me ever in your mind as I offer this gift of loving care to others. In your Son's name. Amen.*

Reading this book, you've already encountered a number of ways of relating to suffering people that build them up rather than tear them down. Caring for suffering people can be challenging, and the message of this book is that it's doable. It's not always easy, but it's very accomplishable.

The seven caring actions in this chapter are "sure winners." Those who participated in our research gave these seven ways of caring universal affirmation. The actions themselves are simple, and when you make a point to include them in your relating at opportune times, they can have a profound effect on those who are hurting.

## GENUINE PRAYER

Martin Luther said the first rule of prayer is, "Don't lie to God." If this is the first rule, then the second is like it: Don't lie to the person you are promising to pray for, either. If you say you are going to pray for someone, make sure you do it. A friend wrote to me after Joan died: "You stay in my prayers daily, Ken. They are real prayers, not just the kind we sometimes say we will offer but don't." I knew this person truly was praying, and I was strengthened by it.

People find great comfort when they know others are praying for them. "When I was in a threatening circumstance, I was so distracted by my pain that I didn't feel as if my prayers were very effective," one person said. "It was such a relief to know that someone else was stepping in to pray on my behalf."

A painfully honest man, however, said the following about those who told him that he would be in their thoughts and prayers: "I appreciate the sentiment but have no expectations that person actually will pray. That's because when I say something similar, I usually forget."

Your sincerity will never be questioned, however, if you are specific about when and how you will pray. "I thought of you three times today," someone told Joan, "and prayed each time that God would enclose you in his love." Another person wrote to her, "Each morning in my prayer time I pray for you. Today God prompted me also to write to you." One friend was very specific with a research participant: "When I pray tonight, I'm going to ask God to walk with you and hold your hand through this difficult time."

Be careful to make sure that talking about prayer—or praying with a hurting person—is appropriate. Someone who is angry at God, for instance, may not want you to pray with him or her. It's always appropriate, however, to pray privately for that person. As one caregiver commented, "While I think praying *for* people in pain is always good, sometimes praying *with* that person is not."

Listening is also a key factor in praying for others. One woman reflected on her thoughts about prayer when she had been suffering: "Prayer without enough listening is not always that helpful. I wanted someone to listen to me first, to know what I needed, and to ask my permission to pray with me. Otherwise, it seemed like they were just doing their duty without having a sincere interest in me and my situation."

Once you determine that praying with an individual is appropriate, the most reassuring way to approach the subject is to ask what the person would like you to pray for. That way, the person you are praying for helps you build the content of your prayer. He or she will know that you are praying specifically about his or her fears, pain, or other needs.

## SHOWING UP

Good caring and relating start with being there for the other person. As simple as this sounds, it's an extremely effective act of caring. One woman whose spouse had died said: "I received phone calls and visits from friends at various times when I was most despondent. I'm not sure how they knew when to call or visit. I think they were sent by God." An impulse like this has probably occurred to you before: "I should go visit so-and-so" or "I should give so-and-so a call." Do it. Take the initiative.

Be careful not to add to the burden of the hurting person, however, by asking him or her to take the first step in getting together as with the typical suggestion: "Let's have lunch sometime." Such a statement leaves the initiative with the other person. Maybe that's fair enough under normal circumstances, but when you say it to a hurting person, you are asking that individual to reach out to you instead of your reaching out to him or her. Imagine how hard it is for the hurting person to take the initiative when most of his or her energy is devoted to coping. It's much better to take the first step yourself by saying something like, "Let's have lunch sometime *next week,* if you can," then propose possible times.

Suffering people value and appreciate your simple act of showing up and being there. The fact that you are willing to take time out of what may have been an otherwise pleasant and pain-free day to share in someone's pain speaks volumes. It communicates that the individual's pain is important to you, that you consider the pain to be real, significant, and close to your heart, and that you care enough to choose to share that person's pain.

## NAMING THE ELEPHANT

Imagine that you and several others are spending an evening at a friend's house. At one end of the living room stands a large elephant. All of you can see it, smell it, even hear it. Yet throughout the entire evening, no one mentions or even acknowledges the presence of the elephant.

No, this is not a scene from the theater of the absurd. Perhaps you have encountered a similar situation where a painful event has happened to someone. You and others know about the crisis or loss, and he or she knows you know. But no one dares mention the one thing the hurting person hopes you'll notice and comment on. There is an elephant in the room, and no one is willing to acknowledge that it's there.

Consider the all-too-common experience of the following people who participated in the research:

- A woman who had experienced a miscarriage said, "People acted as though nothing had happened. They never mentioned it."

- A husband and father who lost his job when the plant where he worked shut down said it was hurtful when people "did not even acknowledge my situation."

- A woman whose daughter attempted suicide said, "I felt as if my pain must have been visible, like it was painted on my chest. I was surprised when people seemed totally oblivious and never said a word."

A simple but very profound act of care that you can offer to a suffering person is to *name the elephant.* Note that this isn't about "naming the mouse" or "naming the pet dog." It's about daring to speak of a glaring and obvious situation or event. Don't ignore it. Don't pretend it's not there. Be sensitive, and name the elephant.

When we were in San Antonio for Joan's treatment, our younger daughter Amity informed us that a friend had been diagnosed with liver cancer. Joan decided to call her. I could only hear Joan's end of the conversation. "This is Joan Haugk," she said. "It's been a while since we've talked." After a few seconds Joan said, "I hear you received some bad news." There was a longer pause, and then Joan said, "That's really terrible. I've been thinking about you for the past two days since I first heard about this." Joan moved the elephant front and center, immediately acknowledging our friend's situation.

The hurting person might also name his or her own elephant before you do. If this occurs, don't just let the person stand there exposed. Be sure to acknowledge the naming. Listen. Make it very clear that you are willing to talk about the person's pain.

When hurting people refer to the situations causing their suffering, they strongly desire to have their pain acknowledged. When you pick up on those cues, you will be the kind of person around whom people feel comfortable naming their elephants.

## REMINISCING

A couple of months after Joan died, I was with our two daughters, son-in-law, and grandson at a restaurant. Our older daughter, Charity, was deliberating between the soup and the salad and asked if she could sample the soup of the day. After the server left to get the sample, our son-in-law, Jamie, smiled and commented that Charity was just like her mother because Joan used to ask to sample the soup before ordering it. The conversation immediately turned to our memories of Joan. My heart was warmed, because Jamie could talk so naturally about Joan.

Grieving people commonly want others to remember their loved one. In fact, this desire was universal in our research. Every person interviewed on this subject wanted others to talk about his or her deceased loved one. One man said, "To mention my wife's name after she died was so hard for some people. It was almost as if she had never existed. I guess they thought talking about her would be too painful for me, but I wanted them to remember her." The simple act of mentioning the name of a deceased loved one acknowledges that the person has not been forgotten and that his or her life carries continued significance. It's a beautifully warm and caring experience, and it's a sure winner when you do it.

Seize the natural opportunities that arise to reminisce with a hurting person. The key word here is *natural*. Share whatever comes to your mind—warm memories, humorous stories, or character traits you admired.

One man said that after his father died, the father's pastor told him specifically about his father's faith and about how proud his father had been of him. "This was a gift, a blessing, since my dad could not communicate so personally with me."

After her mother's death, one woman said that people "shared memories of my mom. They told funny anecdotes or shared the wisdom she had shared with them, telling about the times she had been there for them. It hurt a little at the time, but it was a good kind of hurt. We laughed and cried together over memories of my mom."

Reminiscing is particularly welcome when you're relating to a person whose loved one has died, but people appreciate it in other situations as well. You can reminisce how life was before a major change. For example, a father whose children have moved away may enjoy hearing your memories about his children as they were growing up. Reminiscing with family members whose parent is suffering from Alzheimer's can help them remember the good times with that person.

Reminiscing means sharing your own memories, of course, but it also includes a lot of listening. After you reminisce a while, you may find that the hurting person begins to reminisce, too. Then it's better to listen, even if you have more to share. You can save your additional reminiscing for later.

## ASKING OTHERS HOW THEY ARE DOING

At times of crisis or loss, the person who receives the primary focus of care is usually the one most directly affected, for example, the person who's ill or the spouse of a person who died. While this is certainly appropriate, there are often others also needing care: family members or friends who are very concerned and need someone to listen to their feelings about what is happening.

Consider this example. A woman experiences a miscarriage and is subsequently surrounded and uplifted by the care and concern of family members and friends. Her husband receives some care as well, but the question he's most often asked is "How is your wife doing?" The other children in the family may also be grieving the loss of their anticipated sibling and trying to understand their parents' grief. The question they most often will hear, however, is "How is your mother doing?"

Even though the mother is probably the most directly affected, all the family members are grieving. Yet rarely does anyone ask the others how they are doing. One woman told this story: "After having open heart surgery at 18 months, our daughter had a stroke. She began recovering quickly. Many people would ask how she was progressing and how her heart was, but rarely did anyone take the time to find out how the rest of our family was doing."

Another woman had a different experience: "My sister was dying of cancer. It felt good when people would hug me and let me know they were praying for my sister. It felt even better when they told me they were praying for my strength as well."

Were these people selfish or jealous of the attention paid to the person who was most involved in these tragic situations? Of course not. They just needed someone to acknowledge their pain, too.

You can be the exceptional person—a real hero—who asks these other people how they are doing. It's another sure winner.

## PRACTICAL HELP

Practical help can be a lifeline to someone drowning in a sea of trouble. One woman who faced a terrible tragedy told of the help she received: "People took over daily chores for me because I was numb. Neighbors, church members, and family cooked, cleaned, shopped, ran errands, did everything they could because I could not think clearly. My children were 2, 5, 8, and 10 at the time. Life had to go on, but I just *couldn't* go on. All of those caregivers helped me find the way back."

Most of us instinctively tell a hurting person, "Call me if there is anything I can do to help," and having made the offer, we relax until called. But the call rarely comes. Why? Because, again, the burden of initiating the contact rests with the suffering person. Many times, people simply don't want to impose on others, or they don't like to ask for help. Perhaps the suffering person simply doesn't have the energy or the focus to organize people to help. Because of this, it is much more meaningful to offer to do something specific.

The key question is *What does this person really need?* The key to finding the answer is simple: Ask. If you want to help, make it a point to find out what the other person truly needs instead of assuming you already know. Here's what one recipient of practical help said: "My husband had open heart surgery to repair a defective heart valve—we had one week to prepare. What was so helpful to us were the people who asked what they could do to help and actually listened to my suggestions and did these things." The simple act of asking first ensures that your attempts to provide practical help will meet real needs.

Sometimes, a suffering person cannot think clearly enough to know what needs to be done. At such times be creative in your offers of help. One individual, totally unable to focus on what she had to do after an accident took the lives of several close family members, was astonished and grateful when someone offered to clean and polish all of her family's shoes before they traveled out of state to the funeral.

Research participants listed the most helpful offers of practical help they received in this order:

1. Providing or preparing meals

2. Caring for children

3. Doing household chores

4. Providing transportation

5. Shopping or running errands

6. Caring for pets and other animals

7. Making phone calls

8. Staying with an ill family member so the primary caregiver can attend to other business

They not only mentioned these general categories of helping activities, but they also noted some specific—and special—things you could do to help a suffering person.

**Meals**—Make sure that the family needs the food you are offering and that someone will be home to receive it. Ask if there are any special dietary needs or restrictions. Find out if anyone dislikes a particular food. One pastor wrote about a parishioner who had been the benefactor of many carried-in suppers. "Please tell them not to bring one more congealed salad," the elderly gentleman begged. He truly appreciated the meals but hated gelatin salads. Take food only in disposable containers, so the hurting person does not have to expend energy in returning bowls or plates. *Special gift:* An assortment of disposable plastic containers for storing leftovers.

**Outside Chores**—Mow the lawn, rake the leaves, or wash the car. *Special gift:* Take care of plantings or a garden.

**Hospitalization**—Keep your visits short, ten to fifteen minutes maximum, to avoid tiring the patient. Make sure you are in good health when you visit a patient. Because of limited space in hospital rooms, you may want to wait to send flowers, a plant, or balloons to the patient's home where he or she can enjoy them while recuperating. Pretty cards and notes are best during the hospital stay. *Special gift for a prolonged hospital stay or recuperation at home:* A basket filled with small, wrapped gifts for the patient to open, one each day.

**Funerals**—Offer to care for young children or aged relatives during visitation and on the day of the funeral. You could also arrange for someone to house-sit during the funeral. This can help prevent crime by those who prey on grieving people while they are away from home. *Special gift:* Meet incoming relatives at the airport.

All of these creative ideas could be helpful *if*—and this is a very big "if"—the hurting person and those around him or her really want this particular kind of help. There is a very fine line between helping and intruding, and you need to walk it carefully. Ask questions to discover the best way to relate to and care for someone who is hurting, and then abide by his or her wishes.

## FOLLOWING UP

During the initial time of crisis hurting people are often surrounded by others wanting to help. "But they don't stick around to help pick up the pieces in the long run," one woman in a focus group lamented.

Another agreed: "After the first contact, most never asked again how I was doing."

"There were a few people who lingered for a while," another person said. "They sent cards, cooked meals, gave me hugs. But then after three or four months all of that stops, too."

Another sighed, "And all of the casseroles you had before—you know, six months later one of those might be nice."

All these people were expressing the need for follow-up. A good example of follow-up caring and relating is to recognize certain important anniversary dates—the wedding anniversary of a couple where a spouse has died, the birthday of a loved one who has died, the anniversary date of a person's death. A bereaved person is very likely to experience an upsurge of grief as one of these significant days approaches and would appreciate a note or call.

But follow-up isn't just reserved for the bereaved. Many events transpire that can radically change a person's life and generate long-term effects. These, too, cry out for follow-up. A woman who was divorced after 27 years of marriage expressed great appreciation for the follow-up care she received: "My friends called regularly from New England to my home in Texas for months." A man who had experienced a difficult relocation also found follow-up helpful: "People asked how we were doing and kept on asking even five or six months after the move."

Following up provides the support a hurting person needs, plus it acknowledges the fact that suffering can last a long time.

Simple and profound acts of genuine concern and compassion make a great difference in the lives of those who are suffering and in the lives of those who care for them. In Matthew 25:34–40, Jesus, the King, describes those whom he will welcome into their inheritance:

> "For I was hungry and you gave me something to eat, I was thirsty and you gave me something to drink, I was a stranger and you invited me in, I needed clothes and you clothed me, I was sick and you looked after me, I was in prison and you came to visit me."

The people wonder when they had ever done that for Jesus, and he replies,

> "I tell you the truth, whatever you did for one of the least of these brothers of mine, you did for me."

Simple acts. Profound effects.

# Epilogue
## OUT OF THE FIRE

I began this book by telling you that it comes "out of the fire." It comes out of the fire of my hot sorrow and my resolve to make life more bearable for others who are suffering. It also comes from the fire of conviction. I have been the recipient of some very helpful caring and relating. I have even managed to do the right thing at the right moment myself from time to time. So I am convinced that what I am urging is attainable.

Caring in ways that meet the deepest needs of those who are hurting is within everyone's power. Yours, too, because it's within the power of Jesus Christ who is at work in you and through you.

In the course of the interviews, surveys, focus groups, and other samplings of people's experiences and hopes for their own caring and relating, I asked, "What is your vision for yourself in being able to relate to those experiencing pain and suffering?" Among the many excellent answers I received, one person's vision stands out:

> I am a conduit of grace. As I enter a room, I bring
> the full resources of God's grace with me. My
> vision is to be such a presence that one who hurts
> may drink deeply of this wonderful grace of God.

This person's vision summarizes my hope for you. I hope you will be such a conduit as you encounter hurting individuals. And I hope that people with such a vision will surround you and bear you up when you are in the grip of life's hurts and pains.

Because of your desire to help, not hurt, and your prayerful compassion for others, I know you can be God's grace to those who are suffering. Like the Good Samaritan in Luke 10, you are the one who will stop and give aid to the beaten person by the side of the road. You are the one.

I encourage you to enter into the fire of the suffering of others, to be God's loving presence to them. And so I send you off with this blessing, which has always been especially meaningful for me:

> *May God himself, the God of peace, sanctify you
> through and through. May your whole spirit, soul
> and body be kept blameless at the coming of our
> Lord Jesus Christ. The one who calls you is faith-
> ful and he will do it.*
>
> *—1 Thessalonians 5:23–24*

# NOTES

## Introduction

1 "Helping" from Shel Silverstein, *Where the Sidewalk Ends,* copyright © Evil Eye Music, Inc., 1974; first appearing in *Free to Be . . . You and Me,* copyright © 1972, and used by permission of The Ms. Foundation for Women, Inc.

## Chapter 3

1 C. S. Lewis, *A Grief Observed* (1961; restored, New York: HarperCollins, 1996), pp. 52–53.

## Chapter 4

1 Henri J. M. Nouwen, *The Wounded Healer* (1972; reprint, New York: Doubleday—Image Books, 1990), p. 39.

2 Nouwen, p. 41.

3 Nouwen, p. 63.

4 Nouwen, p. 71.

## Chapter 6

1 Philip Yancey, *Disappointment with God: Three Questions No One Asks Aloud* (Grand Rapids, MI: Zondervan, 1988), p. 235.

2 Terri Green, *Simple Acts of Kindness: Practical Ways to Help People in Need* (Grand Rapids, MI: Fleming H. Revell, 2004), p. 27.

## Chapter 7

1 Henri J. M. Nouwen, *The Wounded Healer* (1972; reprint, New York: Doubleday—Image Books, 1990), p. 90.

## Chapter 9

1 Tertullian, *Apology* 39:7, in *The Faith of the Early Fathers,* selected and trans. W. A. Jurgens (Collegeville, MN: The Liturgical Press, 1972), Vol. I, p. 116.

2 Doug Manning, *Thoughts for the Grieving Christian* (Oklahoma City, Oklahoma: In-Sight Books, 2001), p. 30.

## Chapter 11

1 Carl R. Rogers, *On Becoming a Person: A Therapist's View of Psychotherapy* (Boston: Houghton Mifflin, 1961), p. 34.

2 C. S. Lewis, *A Grief Observed* (1961; restored, New York: HarperCollins, 1996), pp. 10–11.

# Acknowledgments

Authors get the credit for books by having their names on the cover, but in truth a book is a collaborative effort, the product of many helping hands. Certainly this book is such a collaboration.

Research participants lead the list of those deserving my thanks. More than 4,252 people opened themselves willingly in interviews, focus groups, and surveys. Then the completed manuscript was circulated among scores of reviewers from dozens of denominations. I am deeply grateful to all of them.

Three biblical scholars helped me with some theological and exegetical research and later reviewed the entire book: David Bales, Jack Niermann, and Kevin Scott. Their knowledge and perceptiveness contributed significantly to this work.

Four colleagues—Sandy Ashby, Joel Bretscher, Bill McKay, and David Paap—were especially helpful in their commentary. The editing help of Jeanette Rudder and Scott Perry contributed materially to the precision and clarity of the text. I am grateful for their insights. Keeping track of all the research data fell to Lori Kem. Without her steady organizational touch, this project might well have foundered.

Special thanks to the transcriptionists who carefully typed up my notes and the many pages of research material and patiently made multiple changes to each draft of the manuscript—Jill Botsford, Becky Bogar, Nanette Dost, Christine Hansen, Liz Schaus, Patsy Clark, and Meghan Peters.

My grateful appreciation goes to Heidi Dietrich and Sarah Niebling for applying their expertise in graphic design to the covers of this book, and to Heidi, in particular, for her careful typesetting and formatting of every page.

Finally, my two daughters, Charity and Amity, participated in continuing conversations and critiques throughout the three-year duration of this writing, as did Charity's husband, Jamie. Their support and feedback helped me keep the project on a steady keel.

Seeing a book off to the printer is a little like attending the college graduation of one of your children. The book is off into the world, on its own. I hope the world is as glad to welcome this book as I was to write it. I hope it becomes a blessing to the world, as many people have been a blessing to me and those I love.

# ABOUT THE AUTHOR

Rev. Kenneth C. Haugk, Ph.D., a pastor and clinical psychologist, is the founder and Executive Director of Stephen Ministries, a not-for-profit Christian training organization based in St. Louis, Missouri. As a parish pastor in 1975, he realized that the needs for care in his congregation exceeded what he alone could provide, so he drew on his psychological and theological background to train nine members as "Stephen Ministers" to assist him with pastoral care. Later that year he and his wife Joan founded Stephen Ministries to bring this caring ministry to other congregations. Today, thousands of congregations and other ministries are involved, and nearly a half-million lay people worldwide have been trained as Stephen Ministers.

Dr. Haugk has written many books, including the best-selling *Christian Caregiving—a Way of Life, Speaking the Truth in Love, Antagonists in the Church,* and the four *Journeying through Grief* books. He also has developed the courses *Caring for Inactive Members: How to Make God's House a Home* and *Discovering God's Vision for Your Life: You and Your Spiritual Gifts* and has researched and created the *Haugk Spiritual Gifts Inventory.*

Dr. Haugk speaks at conferences and conducts workshops on many of these topics. In 2003 he received the National Samaritan Award from the Samaritan Institute for the significant contributions he has made to the field of caring ministry.

# OTHER RESOURCES BY STEPHEN MINISTRIES

## *JOURNEYING THROUGH GRIEF*

*Journeying through Grief* is a set of four short books by Kenneth C. Haugk that pastors, congregations, organizations, and individuals can share with grieving people at four crucial times during the first year after a loved one has died.

1. *A Time to Grieve,* sent three weeks after the loss
2. *Experiencing Grief,* sent three months after the loss
3. *Finding Hope and Healing,* sent six months after the loss
4. *Rebuilding and Remembering,* sent eleven months after the loss

Each book focuses on the feelings and issues the person is likely to be experiencing at that point in grief, offering care, reassurance, support, and hope. *Journeying through Grief* provides a simple yet powerful way to express ongoing concern to a bereaved person throughout that difficult first year.

Each set of books comes with four mailing envelopes and a tracking card that makes it easy to know when to send each book. Also available is a *Giver's Guide* containing suggestions for using the four books as well as sample letters that can be personalized and adapted to send with each book.

For more information about *Journeying through Grief,* log on to www.grief-books.org or contact Stephen Ministries at (314) 428-2600.

## THE STEPHEN SERIES

The Stephen Series is a complete system for training and organizing lay persons—called Stephen Ministers—to provide one-to-one Christian care to people experiencing grief, divorce, hospitalization, relocation, terminal illness, unemployment, and count-less other life crises or challenges. More than 9,000 congregations and other organizations, representing more than 100 denominations, from across the U. S. and Canada and from 21 other countries have turned to the Stephen Series as a means of multiplying caring ministry.

## THE CHRISTCARE SERIES

The ChristCare Series system pro-vides the training, structure, resources, and ongoing support congregations need to organize a growing ministry of Christ-centered, life-changing small groups. ChristCare Groups empower people for mission by building them up in caring community, by deepening their grasp and living of God's Word, by involving them in prayer and worship together, and by helping them discover their spiritual gifts so they can reach out to a hurting world with Jesus' love.

To find out more about the Stephen Series, the ChristCare Series, *Journeying through Grief,* and the other resources of Stephen Ministries, contact:

Stephen Ministries
2045 Innerbelt Business Center Drive
St. Louis, Missouri 63114-5765
(314) 428-2600
www.stephenministries.org